101 SCHOLARSHIP APPLICATIONS

101 SCHOLARSHIP APPLICATIONS

What It Takes to Obtain a Debt-Free College Education

2024 Edition

Gwen Richardson

 For information address: Cushcity Communications, 14300 Cornerstone Village Dr., Suite 370, Houston, TX 77014.

FIRST EDITION

Cover design by Fran Krailo

ISBN: 978-1737449669

10 9 8 7 6 5 4 3 2 1

Printed in the United States of America

To my daughter, Sylvia,
who inspired me to go the extra mile

TABLE OF CONTENTS

INTRODUCTION

We have all read headlines featuring a fortunate college-bound student who has received $100,000 or more in scholarship awards. Assuming that the scholarships were renewable annually, this amount could easily pay for four years of college at any American college or university. As of October 2022, the cost (including tuition, room and board, and other expenses) to attend Harvard University one of the nation's most expensive and prestigious institutions of higher learning, was over $80,000 per year.[1]

However, these success stories, while inspiring, are the exception, not the rule. They are aberrations among the pool of millions of aspiring college students who submit scholarship applications to the hundreds of companies, foundations, and non-profit groups that offer them. The reality is a much different, and sobering, picture.

According to EducationData.org, as of the fall of 2022, 42.8 million borrowers have federal student loan debt. The average federal student loan debt balance is $37,787, while the total average balance (including private loan debt) may be as high as $40,780.[2] In addition, there are more than 43 million college loan borrowers with $1.6 trillion in student loan debt in the United States alone. The amount exceeds what Americans owe on credit cards or auto loans and trails only mortgages.[3]

Three years before our daughter, Sylvia, was headed for college, we began researching scholarship sources and believed that we were well ahead of the game. We purchased the book titled *Peterson's Scholarships, Grants and Prizes,* a mammoth reference tool of nearly one thousand pages. I personally spent a dozen hours combing through the different sections of the book for scholarships that applied specifically to her field of study (accounting), her state of residence (Texas), and her ethnicity (African-American). Using a highlighter and sticky note tabs as referencing tools, I thought I was well-prepared for the task that lay ahead. Little did I know that the landscape that lay before us would be quite different than we expected.

Scholarships Are Highly Competitive

Our biggest surprise was the level of competitiveness of the scholarships that are offered. The competitiveness of the college application process is well documented and, at many colleges, 10 percent or fewer of the applicants are admitted. The 2018 pool of applicants to Harvard University, for example, was 42,749, with only 1,962 students – or 4.59 percent, who were admitted.[4] The scholarship process is more competitive by far.

Conversely, the Coca-Cola Scholars Foundation received over 93,000 applicants for its 2020 award to 150 student winners. This is a ratio of less than 1 percent.[5]

Other scholarship organizations report similar results. The FedEx Scholarship, administered by the United Negro College Fund (UNCF), received 1,600 applications for only five scholarships, an award ratio of less than 1 percent.

Cast a Wide Net/Apply For *Lots* of Scholarships

With that level of competition, a student must cast a wide net to have a reasonable chance of winning enough scholarships to cover most, if not all, college expenses. That was the impetus behind my choice for this book's title, *101*

Scholarship Applications. Even though our daughter had an exemplary high school academic record -- a GPA of 3.8 on a 4.0 scale, in the top 9 percent of her graduating class, and 300 hours of community service during her high school years -- we had submitted our *seventy-third* scholarship application before we received our first award letter for her freshman year of college.

The letter we received was for a scholarship that had been submitted several months prior to that, but the important thing is that we did not become discouraged during the process. At that point, we had already received about 20 letters of denial or regret, which was a bit disheartening, to say the least. But we continued to submit applications until we started receiving positive results.

With the combination of grants and scholarships, at about the time she moved into her college dormitory for her freshman year at North Carolina Central University, a historically black college/university (HBCU), her entire year's expenses were paid in full. Some of the financial aid was renewable annually as long as she maintained a GPA of 3.0 or better. She graduated four years later with *absolutely no student loan debt.*

Yet, not only will the volume of scholarship applications increase a student's odds of winning, but the exercise itself has merits. As you prepare dozens of submissions, you will hone your skills and your applications will become more and more refined. You will begin to see patterns in the process, which will allow you to anticipate what selection committees expect. And you will begin to accumulate the materials needed, making the process less challenging as the months progress.

Myths About Scholarships

There are several myths about scholarships that will be dispelled in this book.

Myth #1: Only students with high GPAs qualify for scholarships. In actuality, eligibility requirements range from 2.5 to 3.5, with an average of about 3.0. Many scholarships do not require a minimum GPA and are based on other factors, such as community service or an essay competition. In addition, although a limited number of scholarship applications require the inclusion of SAT scores, the scores are primarily utilized for the purposes of confirming that the student took the test. It is rare that a scholarship will have a requirement of a minimum SAT or ACT score.

Myth #2: Only students from low-income households can obtain scholarships. While many scholarships are based on financial need, there are many others that do not take family income into consideration during the process.

Myth #3: Most scholarships are awarded to students from ethnic minority groups. There are many scholarships that are specific to students who are African-American, Hispanic or Asian. However, there are many more scholarships for which ethnicity plays no role regarding eligibility.

Myth #4: Most scholarships are limited exclusively to high school seniors. A student's senior year in high school tends to be when most individuals begin pursuing scholarships, but scholarship funding is available throughout all four years of undergraduate study, as well as during graduate school. In fact, among the scholarships listed in this book, only 20 percent are restricted exclusively to high school seniors. Most are for undergraduates at any level, and about 10 percent are available to students at the graduate level.

Myth #5: The student should be solely responsible for the scholarship application process. A generation ago, the scholarship process was relatively simple. Once a student received acceptance to a college or university, the institution sent a statement reflecting the financial aid for which the student qualified. The statement would include Federal grant programs, school-based financial aid, student loans, and work-study programs. The student simply accepted the financial aid package and everything was handled through the institution.

That is no longer the case. Because the cost of a college education has skyrocketed over the past two decades, colleges usually do not offer enough financial aid to cover all of the expenses, even for those students who qualify. Colleges still send financial aid award letters to those students who meet their eligibility requirements. But individual award letters may include a higher percentage of student loans than scholarships and/or grants, including the Parent Plus loans for a student's parents.

If a student seeks to reduce these expenses by submitting multiple scholarship applications to a variety of sponsoring entities, the amount of time required will be substantial. During high school junior and senior years, students who are high academic achievers will take advanced placement courses in calculus, chemistry, physics, English, and a foreign language, requiring them to spend a significant number of hours in course work and study. The same is true for college students. Participation in extracurricular activities, community service projects, and part-time jobs will also be time-consuming. Most students simply will not have enough hours available in their school day to perform all of the work required for scholarship submissions.

Parental assistance will be required to perform necessary tasks, including, but not limited to, the following:

- Ensuring that all scholarship deadlines are met,
- Retrieving, copying, or scanning necessary documents,
- Editing essays prior to submission,
- Requesting letters of recommendation from teachers and advisers,
- Visiting the high school registrar's office or contacting the college's registrar's office to request official transcripts,
- Following up with scholarship organizations that request additional documents,
- Making sure that any documents the educational institution must complete and submit to the sponsoring organization are completed and submitted by the required deadline,
- Making sure the scholarship funds actually arrive at the financial aid office and are applied to the student's account,
- Contacting scholarship organizations whose websites experience technical difficulties,
- Contacting scholarship organizations whose award checks are for the incorrect amount (this actually happened to us),

- Double-checking scholarship packages to ensure all documents are included prior to mailing or online uploading, and
- Traveling to the post office to mail scholarship packages or other required documents.

Myth #6: A debt-free college education is no longer possible. Based on a January 3, 2018 article in *College Campus Life News* this myth has become widespread. "It's almost unheard of for someone to finance their undergraduate education themselves or through scholarships," writes Lorena Roberts, a reporter for the online publication.[6]

However, a debt-free college education *is* possible. There are a number of factors involved, such as the dollar amount the college charges for tuition and fees; whether the institution is a private one or a public one; whether or not the student attends college in a different state, thus incurring out-of-state fees; the student's declared major; and the amount of effort the student and his/her parents are willing to expend when identifying and applying for scholarships.

The purpose of this book is to assist parents and their college-bound children with the scholarship process and sources for awards. It is information that I wish I had when I first embarked upon my quest for a debt-free college education for our daughter.

It is my and my husband's belief that, once a student graduates from college with a bachelor's degree, he/she should be able to launch a career without being saddled with a mountain of debt that is the equivalent of a mortgage. With the compound interest, penalties and fees assessed, a college loan debt of $40,000 or more can take decades to repay, especially if the individual experiences any periods of unemployment throughout his or her career. In fact, many college loans are now structured with a 25-year payout schedule! Outstanding loan debt in the six-figure range is not uncommon, especially for graduate students.

The days of an individual working for one company for 40 years without interruption are virtually gone for good. This increases the likelihood that, at some time along one's career path, there will be at least one period of unemployment. Our hope is that those who read this book will be able to avoid mounds of college loan debt, and begin their professional lives with a clean financial slate and a favorable credit score.

College students and their parents will most likely experience pressure to borrow money for college – from the institution the student attends, from former students who have debt, and even from family members. If students resist the pressure and eliminate or minimize college loan debt, they will experience the delayed gratification of being debt-free when they graduate.

After conducting several years of research and spending hundreds of hours on the scholarship application process, compiling all of the information into a book seemed appropriate. Once you achieve success by utilizing the tips and strategies included in this book, send an email to me at gwenrichardson123@gmail.com and let me know when your goals have been achieved. I have also created a Facebook page (https://www.facebook.com/debtfreecollegebook) where I post new scholarship opportunities, photos, pertinent news articles, and scholarship success stories.

CHAPTER 1

DEVELOP A PLAN OF ACTION

Before getting started with the scholarship application process, you will need to know the most important factor involved. The answer might surprise you.

In fact, the most important factor is not the student's grade point average, SAT score, or resume; nor is it the level of objectivity among the members of the selection committee, or the comprehensiveness of the scholarship list used as a reference tool. While these factors do play a meaningful role, they are not the most crucial. The most important factor is the level of commitment parents and students bring to the task.

High school students must be committed to putting forth their best effort in their school work; to taking both the PSAT and the SAT tests twice; to participating in appropriate extracurricular activities and community service projects to enhance their academic portfolios; and to associating with other equally-driven, like-minded students who are also preparing for college matriculation. College students must be committed to utilizing effect time management during their course study; maintaining high GPAs; and becoming involved in campus and community activities.

Parents must be committed to motivating and encouraging their children (the students); to conducting much of the research required to identify the scholarships; to performing much of the required leg-work; and to maintaining a continuous, positive attitude, even after the rejection letters begin to arrive. Without the commitment, success will be elusive. But it is better to potentially spend hundreds of hours of diligent work on the front end to secure scholarships for a debt-free college education, than to spend 30+ years repaying the principal and interest on a five- or six-figure college indebtedness.

Cost of College Education

Now, here is some background information on the cost of obtaining a college education. College costs have increased at a rate much higher than the rate of inflation over the past 20 years. The median household income rose by 20.3 percent between 2002 and 2012, the most recent year from which data is available, according to the U.S. Census Bureau. By comparison, during the same ten-year period, the College Board reports that the average cost of tuition, fees, and room and board for an in-state student at a public four-year university rose by 66 percent.[7]

As a result of tuition hikes, educational borrowing has also increased dramatically. In years past, educational borrowing was once capped by law at $4,000 per family per year. The maximum amount a student can borrow for college has risen dramatically.

Undergraduates can borrow up to $57,500 over the course of their college matriculation. No more than $23,000 of this amount may be in subsidized loans. However, this amount may not be enough to cover the cost of undergraduate education. The Parent Direct PLUS Loan was created to cover the shortfall. In other words, rather than the student bear the sole responsibility for student loan debt, parents are now borrowing as well. This puts two generations in debt for the education of a student(s) in a single generation.[8]

For graduate and professional students, the amount that can be borrowed is almost limitless. With Direct PLUS Loans, which do not have any annual or aggregate loan limits, graduate and professional students and parents of dependent undergraduate students can borrow up to the full cost of attendance.[9]
the borrowing limit is higher at $138,500 of which no more than $65,500 may be in subsidized loans. The graduate aggregate limit includes all federal loans received for undergraduate study. Even at a relatively low interest rate, a six-figure debt level will usually take decades to pay in full.

High School Performance Is Important During All Four Years

As with any project or goal, developing a plan of action is the first step. The quest for college scholarships actually starts in the student's ninth-grade year of high school. Students should take the PSAT in both grades 9 and 10 (some students take it in the eighth grade), and the SAT in both grades 11 and 12. The more practice students receive taking these critical exams, the higher their scores will be. There are several books that can be purchased that include sample test questions and students are encouraged to obtain one or more for review purposes. One of the best known books is *The Official SAT Guide*, published by the College Board.

Cumulative grade point averages (GPAs) are assessed from ninth to twelfth grade and every semester counts toward the class rank and overall GPA. Enrolling in either advanced placement (AP) or dual-credit courses while in high school will boost a student's GPA and class rank, if the student receives a grade of C or above. Thus, it is highly recommended that students enroll in at least two or three advanced courses each high school year. Enrollment in advanced courses will help distinguish you from those students who do not, and provide you with an advantage during the selection process.

In addition, preparing more completely for college by taking AP, honors and additional math and science courses in high school tends to result in increased college completion rates. Several studies have shown that completing rigorous academic curricula in high school may also help students overcome a variety of socioeconomic disadvantages.[10]

Some scholarships, such as the Dell Scholars Program, require participation in specific academic programs during both the eleventh and twelfth grades.

If you are a high school junior or senior, you may not have taken the above information into account during your freshman and sophomore years. However, you still have enough time to make adjustments to your curriculum, extracurricular activities, and community service projects.

Regarding the actual scholarship quest, you will need to begin work on your scholarship project at least 12 months in advance of college matriculation, preferably during your junior year of high school. Starting early will give you an opportunity to fully develop your initial database of scholarship opportunities. As you work on your applications, you will identify dozens more along the way, some of which you will decide are too time-consuming, complex, or competitive to pursue.

As stated previously, applicants should be well aware that the pursuit of scholarships is a highly competitive process. Millions of students from across the United States, many of whom are in the top ranks of their graduating classes, will be pursuing the same pool of limited scholarships.

Yet, the competitive nature of the process should not be a deterrent. By submitting dozens of scholarship applications, you can increase the odds that you will receive a few awards of differing amounts. After all, depending upon the scholarship funding level, five or six awards could be enough to pay all of your direct college expenses. Therefore, be sure not to ignore scholarship opportunities that appear to be relatively small – in the $500 to $1,000 range. Applications for the smaller amounts tend to be less cumbersome to complete, and several small scholarships combined can add up to a large amount overall.

Some of the largest scholarship awards come from the colleges and universities themselves. If you have already submitted your college application, or are an undergraduate presently enrolled, the college financial aid office will be the best source for starting your scholarship quest, but they assign and disburse those funds early.

When a university offers a package that is described as a "full ride," many do not include room and board in the package. Room and board costs $7,000 to $10,000 or more per year, depending on the campus. Be sure to ask what's included in the "full ride."

It is a good idea to become acquainted with the head of the institution's financial aid office. Make regular contact with him or her to inquire about new scholarship funds that may have become available. Some students forgo funds because they decide not to accept admission to the institution, or because they receive outside scholarship funding that exceeds their college expenses. These funds are then made available to other needy students. Also, new financial aid funds for students are received by the institution throughout the year. Developing relationships with members of the campus financial aid office staff will keep the student plugged in for any new funding opportunities that arise.

Finally, the initial financial aid award letter you receive from the college of your choice will probably include student loans. However, you are not required to immediately accept the loans. After you receive your scholarship award letters and you are aware of your remaining outstanding balance for the academic year, you can always apply for a college loan then, if necessary.

Influence of Social Media

The influence of social media has become widespread over the past several years and the scholarship process is not immune from the prominence that sites like Facebook, Twitter, and Instagram play in the lives of college-bound students. A number of scholarships include a social media component to the application process. Some of the social media techniques include:

- Requiring applicants to "like" a sponsoring organization's Facebook page,
- Making the popularity of a social media post a factor in advancing applicants to the next level of the competition,
- Creating a video on a specific topic and posting and sharing it via social media,
- Writing 280-character tweets on a specific topic, and

- Posting the scholarship award recipients on the sponsoring organization's Facebook page.

The Dr. Pepper Tuition Giveaway (listed in Chapter 9), for example, requires that applicants create Facebook posts on which the page's fans will vote. Once an applicant has received at least 50 votes, he or she will become eligible to submit a video in the next level of the competition.

As a reflection of the importance of social media in assessing an individual's credibility, some scholarship organizations actually request links to the applicant's social media pages. In other words, sponsoring organizations do not want to be blindsided by awarding a scholarship to someone who may ultimately embarrass the organization because of inappropriate social media posts.

In the coming years, as the popularity of social media continues to increase, more and more organizations will include a social media component in their scholarship application requirements.

Set a Goal

Before beginning your research regarding the various scholarship opportunities that are available, decide what your ultimate goal will be in terms of a dollar amount of scholarship awards. If your goal is to cover all of your college expenses for at least the first school year, then be sure to tally all the applicable costs, including tuition and fees, room and board, and books. The vast majority of scholarships submit the funds directly to the educational institution, referencing the student as the recipient. There are, however, a few scholarships that provide the funds directly to the student to cover related expenses, such as the purchase of a laptop, living expenses, or travel expenses.

There are a sizeable number of scholarships that are only awarded in the sophomore or subsequent years of college and not available to college freshmen. If the student is a graduating high school senior who will be matriculating to college in the upcoming fall, scholarship applications for future years should be maintained separately for submission in later years. Once you complete your first round of scholarship applications for freshman year, you may find that future funds are not needed. This would be a good problem to have!

If you are getting a late start and are already attending college, you still have the opportunity to complete the remainder of your college years without student loan debt. As stated above, there are many scholarships that are available to students during all four years of college, and even some for a fifth year of undergraduate work.

A second step in the planning process is determining how many hours per day or per week you will spend researching scholarship opportunities and submitting applications. As stated previously, in order for this quest to be successful, the student and/or his or her parents must be committed to a consistent regimen.

While working on my daughter's scholarship project, I spent about two hours per day on weekdays, for a total of about 10 hours per week, for at least eight months during her senior year in high school. I believe this is the average amount of time required because of the tedious nature of the work involved. It is a data-driven exercise and also requires an attention to detail and a high level of organizational skills. The amount of time spent continued during her college years to ensure she remained debt-free, although by junior and senior years I was able to cut the amount of time in half.

Since the student's time will be consumed with involvement in academic assignments, community service projects, extracurricular activities, part-time jobs, and preparation for prom and graduation during senior year, I highly recommend that the parent(s) take the lead on the scholarship project. It will allow for the student to submit applications to many more sponsoring organizations than the student could accomplish on his/her own.

Basic information about the student has to be entered repeatedly on both online and paper applications, and it is *not* required that the student personally complete these. The vast majority of scholarship applications are either online forms requiring document uploads, or the documents must be submitted to a specified email address. The essays *are* required to be the student's own work, but parents can help there, too, with editing and refining the finished product.

Finally, you must determine the different avenues that you will utilize for your informational sources. Reference books on scholarship opportunities are a good starting point. But also inquire with your school's guidance counselor, browse websites specializing in scholarships (these will be discussed in detail in Chapter 5), obtain word-of-mouth information from other parents, contact local organizations that offer scholarships, and, most importantly, contact the financial aid office of the intended educational institution once the student has received an acceptance letter. Inquiries via all of these avenues should be made periodically (at least once per month) since new scholarship opportunities are regularly announced to the public.

CHAPTER 2

BE ORGANIZED

As mentioned in Chapter 1, a high level of organization will be required to successfully pursue your scholarship project. Without it, you will not have all of the required documents to accompany your scholarship application, or you will miss scholarship deadlines, resulting in lost opportunities to compete for funds.

The most important aspect of your organizational process is the deadline date for each scholarship. Your data should be placed in order by date with the most imminent deadline at the front of the pile, and then going forward thereafter. Scholarship deadlines are strict; applications are not accepted after the deadline and organizations make no exceptions for late submissions.

For online applications, pay close attention to the time and time zone of the deadline, as well as the date. It is best to submit your application several days in advance of the deadline and not procrastinate until the last minute. However, there may be some instances in which you do not learn about a scholarship until a few days before the submission deadline. The deadline for online submissions is usually midnight, but the time zone could be Eastern, Central, or Pacific. Double and triple check deadline times and dates since, once the deadline passes, your opportunity will have gone with it.

In addition, pay close attention to the eligibility requirements. Some scholarships are only for graduating high school seniors, while others are for those already enrolled in college. Some are for a specific major or have a minimum GPA. Others have a state residency requirement or are restricted to specific educational institutions.

There are a variety of methods one can utilize to maintain the information about potential scholarship opportunities. Some use the spreadsheet method, listing each of the scholarships in an Excel file with separate columns for all of the pertinent information. When my scholarship quest first began, I attempted to use this method. But I quickly discovered that the spreadsheet was inadequate for the voluminous information needed to stay abreast of each program and its requirements.

Instead, I opted for the traditional file folder system, creating a file folder for each scholarship with a label on the tab. When I found information online about the scholarship, I printed the instructions and/or the application and put them in the folder. Email communications were printed and included, and letters received or sent via snail mail were also included.

In addition, I used a Post-it note on the front of each folder, listing the deadline date, the sponsoring organization, and the documents required for submission. As each document was acquired, it was placed in the folder and scratched off the list, until all documents were obtained. Using this system, I always knew which documents were outstanding, and I was constantly aware of the looming submission deadline.

I did, however, create an Excel file to alphabetically list each scholarship application which we completed and submitted, along with the award amount, deadline date and submission date. I did this to avoid duplicating effort and creating files for scholarships for which we had already applied.

Most scholarships require all documents to be submitted online and uploaded to the sponsoring organization's website, or forwarded via email. A small but sizeable percentage of scholarships require that all documents be submitted via U.S. mail. For those that are mailed, usually the package must be *postmarked* by the deadline date, but sometimes the package must be *received* by the deadline date. Make sure you include the distinction between the two in your notations. Allow at least two weeks for packages to arrive via snail mail, unless you pay for expedited delivery via FedEx, UPS or the U.S. Postal Service with a guaranteed delivery date.

There are also scholarships that give applicants the option of submitting packages either online *or* via U.S. mail, but these tend to be relatively few in number.

For online applications, if recommendation letters are required, the entire process is automated. The sponsoring organization will require that the recommender complete and submit the form on the scholarship web site. The applicant submits the name and email address of the individual(s) who will submit the recommendation, and that person receives a direct email notification.

However, teachers and counselors will often have dozens of students requesting recommendations and the deadlines can easily slip through the cracks. I found this to be one of the most challenging aspects of the online submission process. Recommenders must be respectfully nudged along during the process, since they have no incentive to fit these tasks into their schedule other than their willingness to assist the student. Checking the scholarship submission website daily, only to see that the last recommendation form must be submitted before the application is concerned to be complete, can be frustrating.

It is the applicant's responsibility to make the requests early (at least two weeks before the deadline), and follow up with the recommender to ensure that forms are submitted on time. Develop a list of individuals who are willing to be recommenders and spread the work around to avoid overburdening one or two people. Ask at least double the amount required. Avoid the sheer disappointment of having all of your documents submitted on time, yet having the organization reject the application simply because one recommender forgot to submit his or her online form.

Develop a Team of Recommenders

As college students and parents pursue scholarships, it is very important to develop a team of reliable recommenders that you can call on in a pinch. You should never wait until the last minute to submit applications or notify teachers, community service mentors or employers that recommendation letters are needed. But many scholarships now require the entire process to be completed online, which means recommenders actually have to create an account, log on, and submit the recommendation on the sponsoring organization's website. If the recommender fails to follow through, the application will be null and void even if all other parts of the application have been completed.

We actually had a crisis like this during the summer before our daughter's sophomore year in college where a recommender failed to complete the process and was on vacation as the deadline loomed large. Because we had a team of recommenders -- people who were invested in our daughter's college success -- we were able to call on one of them to complete the process and he came through. (By the way, our daughter actually won that scholarship so having the team of recommenders is extremely important.) When there are thousands of dollars at stake, one mistake can mean the difference between college loan debt and a debt-free college education.

CHAPTER 3

REVIEW RESPONSES TO FREQUENTLY ASKED QUESTIONS ABOUT THE SCHOLARSHIP PROCESS

After you have conducted your research and submitted your scholarship applications, the waiting begins. But, before you get started, be aware of the responses to the following frequently asked questions.

How much time does it take to complete a scholarship application?

The amount of time required varies widely from one scholarship opportunity to another. A few scholarship applications take 30 minutes or less to complete, although these are definitely in the minority. Others take several hours or days as information may need to be gathered from a variety of sources and signatures obtained. Be prepared to spend at least two hours completing each scholarship application.

Am I required to pay an application fee for a scholarship?

A few non-profit organizations require that an application or processing fee be paid, but these requests tend to be rare for legitimate scholarships. There are some organization's that require a student to be a member in order to apply for scholarships, which means the annual membership fee must be paid prior to submitting an application. Before paying the membership fee, be sure the organization is reputable and actually dispenses scholarship funds to students each year.

If an individual or company requires you to pay a finder's fee for a scholarship search, this is usually a red flag for a scam. Be leery about individuals or companies who want to serve as middlemen between you and your scholarship funding or who claim to guarantee a scholarship award. No third party can guarantee that a student will receive a scholarship award.

You may receive solicitations from organizations requesting that you pay a membership fee, after which you will become "eligible" for college scholarships. These solicitations are usually scams, designed to prompt you to pay the membership fee, but the scholarships never or rarely materialize.

In addition, beware of "informational" seminars that claim to provide expertise on college financial aid. Although some of these can be legitimate, be aware that they tend to offer few specifics, and are primarily designed to serve as vehicles to pitch high-priced scholarship services.[11]

How long will it be before I am notified about the scholarship award?

The length of time each organization takes to notify scholarship applicants of their decision varies widely from one sponsor to another. In general, the length of time is directly related to the complexity of the application, the number of applicants, and the number of accompanying documents required.

Scholarships that are based solely on an essay will usually make a decision within about 30 days after the deadline. For others with more complex packages, a decision is usually made within 60 days after the deadline. However, many scholarships take much longer – four to five months is not uncommon.

About half of the positive scholarship award notifications for which we applied did not arrive until after fall college classes had already begun. If the student has a letter in hand announcing that he or she is a recipient of an award, the college admissions or registrar's office will usually accept this as an official notification that the funds are forthcoming.

How will I be notified of the selection committee's decision?

The method of notification depends upon the organization, as each organization is different. In general, these are the methods of communication:

- By telephone, followed by a formal letter via snail mail or email,
- By email,
- By snail mail, or
- No notification at all

In some instances, the selection process will go through several rounds. There will be a group of finalists selected and a telephone or in-person interview is conducted before the final decision is made.

Many of the sponsoring organizations only make direct contact with those who receive awards. For these organizations, their websites will usually indicate an expected date when the award is to be announced. If you do not hear from the organization by that date, assume that you are not an award recipient. If a sponsoring group does not indicate a specified announcement date, visit the group's website periodically. Usually, the award recipients are posted there or on their Facebook page.

Receiving rejection letters and emails is part of the process of submitting scholarship applications, but reading these communications is never an enjoyable experience. Yet, with the number of applications you will need to submit to achieve your goal of a debt-free college education, you will receive dozens of letters that begin with "Thank you for submitting your scholarship application. We regret to inform you. . ." You must take all of this in stride and not let these letters discourage nor deter you from your primary objective.

Does the sponsoring organization explain why I did not receive the scholarship?

Unfortunately, no. The organization does not usually provide an explanation, other than to state that there was a lot of competition for only a few slots. The decisions of selection committees are final and are not subject to appeal. However, you have nothing to lose by writing a letter or sending an email requesting feedback, which could be helpful especially if you plan to reapply in the future.

What happens if my scholarship funding exceeds the amount due to the school in tuition, fees, room, board and books?

If the student already has financial aid in place to cover all expenses, the institution may reduce the funding of some school-sponsored grants and scholarships if additional scholarship funds are rewarded. Remember: The vast majority of scholarship checks (about 90 percent) are made payable directly to the institution and funds are sent to the school's financial aid office. Some scholarships will require the student to certify that there is still unmet financial need before forwarding the payment to the school. If all college fees have been paid in full, the scholarship may be awarded to another student who has outstanding financial obligations.

If a student has received a Federal Pell Grant, the amount of funding is usually the same each year as long as the student maintains a specified minimum GPA and the family's financial resources have not dramatically changed.

If the student has already acquired student loans that have been applied to the student's school account, the institution may issue a refund check directly to the student for the amount in excess of tuition, fees, and room and board. Policies differ from one institution to another, so it is best to check with the college financial aid office for clarification regarding excess funds.

For those scholarships where the funds are awarded directly to the student, these funds may be retained by the student for books and other school-related expenses, as long as this is permitted based on the scholarship guidelines.

Do I need to submit 100+ applications every year of college matriculation?

The number of applications submitted depends upon how much time the parent and student devote to the process. You may be among the fortunate families whose college students receive a full-ride for four years, or submit only a few scholarship applications each year and attended college debt-free.

Our experience, however, was different. For the first two years of our daughter's college matriculation, we submitted close to 100 applications. But for both the junior and senior years we found that the award amounts increased within her discipline (accounting), and the requirements were more precise. This meant that the level of competition was not as great and her award percentage increased.

For her junior year we submitted 40 applications and by senior year the number was down to only 25. The funds for the entire academic year were received earlier. For junior year, all funds were received by January of the spring semester. For senior year, all funds were received by August before the academic year began. Both years her scholarship award dollars actually exceeded the maximum amount her university could accept for her expenses. For junior and senior years, the GPA requirements for scholarships tend to be 3.0 or greater so the student will need to keep that in mind to maintain a debt-free status throughout the college years.

Are there strings attached to scholarship awards?

Many corporations provide scholarships to students as a way of giving back to their local communities, or to maintain reputations as good global citizens, or to groom future potential employees within their industries, or simply because it is good public relations to do so. As a general rule, scholarships do not have strings attached to them in terms of the student having to claim fealty to a particular political philosophy or corporate identity.

If a scholarship is renewable, the student may be required to maintain a minimum GPA. A few scholarships will require students to attend a leadership conference, serve as mentors to future scholarship recipients, or participate in an internship program. The vast majority of scholarships, however, do not require that the student perform any activities after the scholarship has been awarded.

Are scholarship funds taxable?

Scholarship funds are *not* taxable if they are used to pay for tuition and fees (books, supplies and equipment) for course work for individuals who are candidates for degrees at a college or university. Scholarship funds *are* taxable if they are stipends, or are used to pay for room and board.[12]

However, a student claimed as a dependent can receive a yearly income up to $12,200 (as of 2019) without owing federal income tax. This should cover at least one semester of room and board at most institutions. For students who are not claimed as dependents, a yearly income up to $12,000 can be earned without owing federal income tax.

For Pell Grants and other Title IV need-based education grants, they are tax free as long as they are used for qualified education expenses (as stated above) during the period for which a grant is awarded. Borrowers of federal and private education loans may deduct up to $2,500 in interest as an above-the-line exclusion from income, even if the taxpayer does not itemize. Please keep these stipulations in mind regarding filing tax returns and reporting income.

What about student loan debt forgiveness or cancellation?

Due to the Covid-19 pandemic, the federal government placed a pause on all student loan payments and accrued interest from March 2020 until September 2023. During this pause, making continued payments was a wise choice. Your outstanding balance was not accruing interest which means that, once outstanding interest fees were paid, all of your payments would go toward the principal. This will allow you to pay off your loan balance much faster than before.

At the time this edition goes to press, President Biden has proposed cancelling up to $20,000 in student loan debt for students whose annual income is less than $125,000. However, this proposal has been challenged in federal and state courts and appears to be unlikely to take effect.

It would be unwise to depend on student loan debt cancellation as a means to lower or limit your debt total. Being debt-free from college loans cannot be based on hope; debt-freedom must be the result of a well-executed plan. Pursuing the goal of a debt-free college education means your financial future is in your own hands, not based on the edicts of politicians. You will be the captain of your own fate toward the ultimate goal of financial freedom.

CHAPTER 4

COLLECT THE REQUIRED DOCUMENTS

Scholarship applications require a variety of supporting documents, some of which will be requested for the majority of package submissions. Some documents are requested less often, depending on the needs of the organization. It is very important that the information included in the documents is accurate and truthful, since inaccurate or false responses are grounds for immediate elimination from the process. For some scholarships, the submission of false information, if discovered prior to the dispersal of funds, can result in the scholarship award being rescinded.

After spending several years submitting hundreds of scholarship applications, I have compiled a comprehensive listing of the documents that were required. The most commonly requested items are listed first.

- Applicant's personal information (legal name, permanent address, phone number, email address, date of birth, social security number)

- Information about applicant's high school (name of school, address, phone number, email address, fax number, principal's name, guidance counselor's name and email address), or college

- Information about applicant's parents (both parents' names, address, phone numbers, email addresses, social security numbers, places of employment, job titles, educational attainment, income)

- Applicant's school performance (dates of attendance, class rank, number of graduates in class, GPA, courses taken, grades in each course).

- Applicant's transcript (Official transcripts must be submitted directly from the educational institution. Some scholarships accept unofficial transcripts, with official ones needed only if applicant is awarded the scholarship or is a finalist.)

- Applicant's SAT or ACT scores (official printout from College Board showing date(s) taken and scores in critical reading, math and writing). PDF format of scores is required for some online applications. The majority of scholarships do *not* include SAT/ACT scores as one of their eligibility requirements.

- Applicant's resume, listing career objective, employment record, honors and awards, extracurricular activities, and community service projects. A one-page resume is preferred. Continue to update the resume as the student's career advances and/or evolves.

- Copy of parents' tax returns for the preceding tax year, being sure to blackout social security numbers (Some applications require tax returns for multiple years, but this is rare.)

- Student's digital photo, usually a head-and-shoulder shot of student only. Some scholarships require submission of an actual glossy photo via snail mail.

- Copy of applicant's birth certificate, passport or naturalization papers (for proof of U.S. citizenship)

- Copy of FAFSA Student Aid Report (SAR) indicating expected family contribution (EFC) (explained in more detail in Chapter 6)

- Copy of college acceptance letter; address and phone number of institution

- Contact name, address and phone number for financial aid and/or admissions office at college which student plans to attend

- Federal school codes for the institution(s) to which student has been accepted

- Recommendation letters from teachers, counselors, advisors, or other individuals who can assess the student's overall performance. Most scholarships require at least two recommendations, but it is suggested that five be obtained to cover all contingencies. Each year, you will need to receive updated recommendation letters from instructors at the student's existing educational institution to maintain current items within your records. (Note: Recommendation letters from relatives are not allowed. Some organizations require that the letters be in separate, sealed envelopes.)

- Names, email addresses, and phone numbers of individuals who submit recommendations (required for some applications submitted entirely online)

- Certification of community service hours expended during high school or college. Some scholarships include pre-printed forms that must be completed; some require a letter from a leader of the organization for which hours were performed; others require online submission of certification.

- Applicant's personal statement, about 250 words in length. This is the basic essay that introduces the student to the sponsoring organization and includes information about family background, school performance, extracurricular activities, career goals, community service activities, and the reason why student is applying for the scholarship. (More information about the all-important essay is included in Chapter 7.)

Make sure that all documents are in clean, smudge-free condition, accurate and factually correct. Elicit the assistance of an English teacher or trained editor to review the student's personal statement to ensure it is grammatically correct, succinct, and error-free.

CHAPTER 5

VISIT IMPORTANT ONLINE SCHOLARSHIP SOURCES

There are many websites that offer assistance with scholarship identification and acquisition. The best scholarship websites have updated information and regularly post new scholarship opportunities. During the years we spent researching and pursuing scholarships, the following were the ones we found to be the most comprehensive and helpful:

Cappex.com (www.cappex.com) describes itself as "your college decision headquarters," the place to discover new colleges and scholarships, compare your top choices and make the decisions that give you peace of mind. Students create a log-in account and enter basic information so scholarship opportunities can be efficiently matched.

The **College Board** (www.collegeboard.org) is a mission-driven not-for-profit organization that connects students to college success and opportunity. The College Board administers the SAT and Advanced Placement testing programs, but its web site also lists scholarship opportunities.

Fastweb.com (www.fastweb.com) is the premier online resource for paying and preparing for college. Fastweb members are matched to relevant scholarship opportunities completely free of charge. With roughly 1.5 million scholarships worth more than $3.4 billion, there are scholarships for *every* student's educational goals, activities and interests. Students create a log-in account and enter basic information so scholarship opportunities can be matched efficiently.

Fastweb.com also publishes interesting articles that include information that is relevant for college students.

You may remember seeing Chris Gray, creator of the **Scholly** phone app (www.myscholly.com), during his appearance on ABC's "Shark Tank." Gray landed a deal from investors Daymond John and Lori Greiner and, since then, Scholly has grown to be one of the top apps in both the iOS App Store and the Google Play Store. The company was named in Inc. Magazine's Top College Start Ups, won Under Armour's Cupid's Cup competition, and won Steve Case's Rise of the Rest Competition.

Thurgood Marshall College Fund (TMCF) (www.tmcf.org) is one of the nation's largest organizations exclusively representing the Black college community. To date the organization has awarded more than $250 million in such assistance to its students and member-schools. TMCF distributes 98 percent of its awards exclusively to HBCUs and Black colleges.

The team of scholarship researchers at **Unigo.com** (www.unigo.com) has created a successful data management and research process. The company believes that the accuracy of the records housed in its award database is the cornerstone upon which its service is built, and works year-round to maintain accurate award information. The team works closely with scholarship providers to ensure that students using the site receive current and accurate scholarship information–and the scholarships in its database have been submitted or verified by the actual award providers.

The **United Negro College Fund (UNCF)** (www.uncf.org) is the nation's largest and most effective minority education organization. Since its founding in 1944, UNCF has raised more than $3.6 billion to help more than 430,000 students receive college degrees at UNCF-member institutions and with UNCF scholarships. Students create a log-in account and enter basic information so scholarship opportunities can be efficiently matched. The website only lists scholarships that are actively accepting applications, so check about once monthly to see which new ones have been listed.

CHAPTER 6

UNDERSTAND THE IMPORTANCE OF THE FAFSA SCORE

The Free Application for Federal Student Aid, also known as FAFSA, is the vehicle through which the Federal government determines which students receive Federal financial aid in the form of grants, loans, and work study. Administered by the U.S. Department of Education, FAFSA is also the yardstick by which most college financial aid offices and several sponsoring organizations determine which students should receive financial aid, as well as the appropriate amount. It is an essential part of the scholarship application process.[13]

The FAFSA application is available online each year after January 1, and should be completed by the student or parent as soon as possible thereafter. Completing and submitting the application is free and quick, and gives students access to the largest source of financial aid to pay for college, vocational school, or graduate school.

Students are able to file their FAFSA applications as early as October 1 for the following academic year. This means they will no longer have to wait for their W-2s to arrive before they get started, and can get a jump on the college application process.[14]

For the most part, the FAFSA utilizes the information on the parents' federal income tax return to assess a student's eligibility for financial aid. It takes into account the student's and parents' income and assets, household size, and the number of family members attending college.[15]

Once the FAFSA has been processed, the student receives an Expected Family Contribution (EFC), which essentially means the amount that parents are expected to be able to pay towards their child's college education. A low EFC score, or dollar amount, means parents can afford to pay very little. A high score, or a relatively high dollar amount, means the parents have an above-average income, and the student will probably not qualify for most Federal financial aid programs.

Financial aid experts consider middle income to be between $40,000 and $65,000.[16] If your family's income exceeds $70,000, your FAFSA or EDC score probably will not be beneficial to you during the scholarship application process. College and university financial aid offices, in particular, rely heavily on the EDC to determine which students receive grants, scholarships and work study.

If your family income increases significantly from one year to the next, your EDC score will increase, which will most likely lead to a decrease in funding for federal educational grant programs. Conversely, if your family income *decreases* substantially from one year to the next, your EDC score will *decrease*, resulting in an *increase* in funding.

If your family has an above-average income, all is not lost. Not all scholarships are based on financial need. For those funded by entities other than the Federal government, such as corporations and non-profit organizations, many are, instead, based on other factors, such as academic performance, demonstrated leadership ability, exemplary community service, a winning essay, an impressive resume, a witty idea, or social media prowess.

For the hundreds of scholarship applications we submitted, only about 20 percent requested a copy of the FAFSA or EDC report. Another handful of scholarships had their own financial forms to be completed. The remainder requested no financial information at all, but some requested an explanation of why the student deserved to receive the scholarship as part of an essay.

CHAPTER 7

CREATE THE ALL-IMPORTANT ESSAY

The quality of the scholarship essay is one of the greatest determining factors for the majority of scholarship evaluations. Regardless of the subject matter included in the essay, it should be well written and grammatically correct. But it should also be succinct, unique, and compelling.

The scholarship process would be much easier for students if one essay would suffice for all scholarship applications. Unfortunately, that is not the case. Your basic essay, which will be your personal statement, can be utilized for a large number of scholarship applications. But even the personal statement will need to be tweaked and adjusted to suit the specific requirements of each sponsoring organization.

The selection committee will be looking for originality, creativity, proper spelling, punctuation, and grammar in your essay. It should be positive, hopeful and forward-looking. Also, pay close attention to the specific details about the essay, such as minimum or maximum word count, number of pages, line spacing, and font size.

Elements of the Personal Statement Essay

The personal statement essay will range between 200 to 500 words, depending on the scholarship requirements, and should include the following information:

- Your name, city of origin, name of your high school or college, and year when you graduated or expect to graduate

- A summary of your GPA, class rank (if favorable), extracurricular activities, honors, and awards

- Leadership activities and positions while in high school or college. If you have started a worthwhile school or community organization, provide details about why and how you established it.

- Information about your intended major or field of study, how you became interested in the field, and your career goals

- Information about your family background and how it has affected your educational goals and attainment

- Your personal interests and hobbies, special skills, and talents

- Your involvement in community service projects, the nature of the projects, and the number of hours expended

- How you expect to use your major after graduation

- Your long-term career goals – Where do you see yourself career-wise in five years? Ten years?

- The reason why you wanted to attend college and why you deserve to receive the scholarship

- The effect that receiving the award will have on your current and future career plans

Your personal statement essay should always be typewritten, repeatedly massaged and reviewed until it is *perfect*. Elicit the assistance of your English teacher or a family member with strong English skills to assist you in the process. If one of the student's parents possesses strong English skills, this is a tremendous plus. Read the essay aloud to make sure it is interesting and flows smoothly. Revised it as your life's circumstances change and new information, such as extracurricular activities or honors, becomes relevant. The importance of the personal statement essay cannot be over-emphasized.

Expect a Variety of Essay Topics

Many scholarship sponsoring organizations have moved beyond the personal statement essay and have become creative about developing their own specific essay topics. Some are based on the industry in which the entity is positioned; others are based on the student's familiarity with current events or economic trends. Some essays require research on a specific topic, or that they be prepared according to a particular format (e.g., Modern Language Association [MLA] format). Some organizations even seem to be attempting to get student applicants to point them in the direction of the next major market trend, to avoid paying a marketing consultant to do it for them.

During your scholarship quest, you will encounter essay topics that seem to reoccur. For essay topics that you encounter repeatedly, retain the narrative you create for future use. That way, you will not be required to reinvent the wheel each time.

Following are examples of some of the requested essay topics we encountered when we researched scholarship applications:

- How does having purpose affect the quality of your life?
- Why should young people get involved in politics?
- If you had the authority to change your school in a positive way, describe the specific changes you would make.
- Given that you already have the necessities for college, if you could only take what fits into a backpack, what would you bring?
- What do you think the status of the Internet will be in five years? What kind of technology will incorporate Internet access?
- Pick a controversial problem on high school or college/university campuses and suggest a solution.
- How can the Web give a company a competitive advantage?
- Every generation faces new challenges and new problems. What do you think is the biggest difference between your generation and older generations?

- How do you define success and what are your plans to be successful?

- What would you do if you were appointed as chair of a non-profit organization and funded $100,000,000?

- Share a story about how language has helped you express your voice.

- Write about a situation where better safety procedures would have prevented an injury.

- How do you use technology to keep your family connected?

- Explain how you go about honoring America's military heroes.

- Name America's most inspirational military leader and why you believe this individual inspires others.

- Explain how your college experience is or will be enabled by remarkable frugality, ingenuity or thrift.

- How do you consider yourself to be more than just a student?

- Define each of the following competencies and their relative importance to you as you navigate through college and prepare to enter a global society: Cross-cultural aptitude, digital literacy, and financial acumen.

- What do I consider a meaningful contribution, by a citizen, to our society? What will I contribute?

- Consider your favorite quotes, books, movies, music, works of art, etc. Have these influenced your life in a meaningful way?

- What does a credit score mean to you and how do you think you will use it in the future?

- How would you address the issue of United States congressional gridlock?

- How has the Internet helped you with your education?

- If you could start one business to benefit mankind, what would it be and why?

As you can see, the potential essay topics run the gamut, so be prepared for just about any topic you can imagine. With careful planning and time management, the essay submission process will be less cumbersome. Do not procrastinate and wait until the last minute to write your essays. Allow at least a week to prepare a rough draft and finalize the essay to be submitted. Then make plans to submit your application, including the essay, at least a week ahead of the deadline.

In many cases, all or part of one essay can be used for multiple scholarship submissions. Sponsoring organizations require that the essay be original, but most do not require that it be exclusive. This means that as long as the essay represents the student's own work, it can be submitted with numerous scholarship applications.

CHAPTER 8

GET SCHOLARSHIP SPONSORS TO NOTICE YOUR APPLICATION

Due to the competitive nature of the scholarship process and the sheer volume of applications that sponsoring organizations receive, it is imperative that your package stand out among the rest. Be aware of your strengths and unique qualities and develop a high-quality presentation that will catch the selection committee's attention.

During the years that we submitted applications, we found that scholarships that required applicants to mail in their packages presented the best opportunity for leveling the playing field. Mailed-in applications allow the student to include additional items that could separate him or her from the pack. The landscape, however, has changed and the vast majority of scholarship applications are now submitted online—not via snail mail.

Unless the organization provides a list of requested items and specifically states, "only include these items and no others," (or something to that effect), the student is presented with an opportunity to include additional attention-getting items. In our case, we had prepared a professional resume and attached a photography studio head shot. If the scholarship requested two recommendation letters, we included four if including more was an option. A copy of an award certificate for exemplary academic performance or community service would be another item that would stand out. An original poem written by the student could be an extra item, especially if the scholarship is based upon creativity. If the student received national recognition for exceptional achievements, this information should be highlighted. Be careful not to load too many additional items in the package, but including one or two that can help make the package distinctive can only be a plus.

Many scholarships allow for or even require video submissions as substitutes for or in addition to essay submissions. The video submissions are usually optional, but I believe that, in a competitive environment, a student who submits an essay *and* a high-quality video increases his/her odds of being noticed.

Be sure to read eligibility requirements carefully. There's no point in applying for a scholarship that you are not eligible to receive. If you are uncertain, contact the sponsoring organization.

The more narrow the parameters for the scholarship application, the greater your odds of success. Scholarships that are open to all high school seniors or college students nationwide will have a large pool of applicants and will be extremely competitive. However, scholarships that are more specific, based on a particular major of study, a small segment of the general population (e.g., based on ethnicity), an individual state or a particular college, will have relatively fewer submissions and will not be as competitive.

Some applicants make the mistake of pursuing only the scholarships offering large dollar amounts. Doing so is similar to buying a lottery ticket. Hundreds of thousands of students are chasing the same high-dollar scholarships which provide a full-ride for four years (like the Gates Scholarship), that pay $20,000 total over a six-year period (like the Dell Scholars Program), or that pay $10,000 per year for four years (like the Ron Brown Scholars Program).

As stated previously, it is important to submit as many scholarship applications as possible to as many organizations as possible. The $500 and $1,000 scholarships may seem to be relatively small amounts, but receiving several scholarships at that funding level may provide the cumulative amount you will need to attend college debt-free.

Crowdfunding As An Option

If you are unable to raise the entire amount of college funds needed through the scholarship process, don't despair. The Internet has offered a novel way to raise money, known as crowdfunding. Thousands of individuals have utilized this avenue to finance all sorts of projects, causes, and, yes, college educations.

Put the power of your network of family (both immediate and extended), friends, and social media followers to work and create your own personal scholarship through crowdfunding. By accumulating small donations from lots of people, you may be able to raise the funds required to finance your education.

There are several websites that have been designed specifically for this purpose, including, GoFundMe.com, Indiegogo.com, and Instagrad.

Through **GoFundMe.com**, students can utilize the crowdfunding platform to create a personal donation campaign, share it online, and use the funds raised.[17] The funds can be used for college expenses and even for repaying student loans. This platform claims to be number one in college tuition fundraising.[18]

There is no fee to set up a campaign; however, GoFundMe.com takes 2.9 percent for processing fees. In addition, there is a fee of $0.30 per transaction.[19]

YouCaring.com has a 120-day limit on the length of fundraisers, but you can run as many as you want. It is possible to get daily access to your funds, so you can apply money toward college expenses or student loans as you go.[20]

Indiegogo.com allows students to raise money for whatever they choose. Students can create a campaign, promote it, and watch their money grow.[21]

Be sure to use the funds for the purpose that is advertised. It would be tragic and deceptive for a student to raise money for education through crowdfunding, but not enroll in school, and then use the funds for some other purpose (e.g., to buy a car or go on a vacation). Make your supporters proud of you and glad that they contributed to your success. But keep in mind that your crowdfunding campaign may be unsuccessful.

Internships

Internships provide another avenue to earn funds for college. While some internships offer only course credit and do not provide monetary compensation, many of them include paid stipends, housing and even salaries. Explore your internship options with companies within the industry you are targeting for your career. Internships enhance students' resumes and give them a leg-up when competing for full-time employment upon graduation. More detailed information about internships is included in Chapter 11.

CHAPTER 9

SUBMIT SEPTEMBER - FEBRUARY SCHOLARSHIP APPLICATIONS

No book that provides guidance regarding the scholarship application process would be complete without a comprehensive listing of scholarship sources. In keeping with this book's title, more than 101 scholarship opportunities are listed in Chapters 9 and 10.

The scholarships listed here can all be applied for directly by the student. They do not require students to go through their high school's guidance counselor or college financial aid office. The links provided go directly to the scholarship page on the organization's web site, whenever possible. Inclusion of these direct links will substantially reduce the amount of time required to search for the specific scholarship and its supporting information. Requirements for each scholarship are listed as bulleted items for easy scanning.

Excluded from this listing are the following categories of scholarships:

- Those based on athletics or participation in team sports;
- Those that require membership in a particular organization or a corporate fee-based membership program;
- Those based upon sweepstakes and random drawings;
- Those based on team projects or competitions; and

- Those that require travel to a particular locale to participate in an oratorical or competitive process in order to receive the award.

The scholarships included in this guide are based on the student's desire for higher education, academic performance, financial need, community service participation, leadership skills, creativity, and/or witty ideas.

Finally, scholarship deadlines are based on the specific dates designated for the 2023-2024 academic year. **It is possible that some of the dates may shift slightly, so checking the sponsoring organization's web site for confirmation of the deadline date is highly recommended.**

YEAR-ROUND OR RECURRING

CDW Legacy Excellence Program Scholarship
Deadline: Varies

Award Amount: $5,000

No. of scholarships: 20

Website:
https://www.cdw.com/content/cdw/en/about/overview/diversity-and-inclusion/hbcu-partnership-programs.html

Requirements:

- College undergraduate student
- Attending a Historically Black College or University (HBCU) or a Predominantly Black Institution (PBI)
- Minimum 3.0 GPA
- Demonstrate financial need

Central Intelligence Agency (CIA) Undergraduate Scholarship Program

Deadline: Applications accepted year-round

Award Amount: Up to $18,000 per calendar year

No. of scholarships: Varies

Website:
https://www.cia.gov/careers/student-programs

Requirements:

- U.S. citizen
- 18 years of age or older by April 1 of senior year in high school
- High school senior planning to enroll in a four- or five-year degree program; or college freshman or sophomore enrolled in a four- or five-year degree program
- Minimum SAT of 1500, ACT of 21
- Minimum 3.0 GPA
- Demonstrate financial need with household income below $70,000 for a family of four
- Available to work in Washington, DC area during summer
- After college graduation, agree to continue employment with CIA for a period equal to 1.5 times the length of college sponsorship

Pulse of Perseverance Monthly Scholarship

Deadline: First day of every month

Award Amount: $1,000

No. of scholarships: 1 per month

Website:
https://www.thepulseofp3.com/scholarship-info-and-winner

Requirements:

- High school student (to assist families with education-related expenses, such as school fees, school supplies, uniforms, college application fees)
- College student (to assist with education-related expenses, such as books, fees, advance degree applications)
- Applicants must read the book, *Pulse of Perseverance: Three Black Doctors on Their Journey to Success* and submit an essay about the book

SEPTEMBER

Andrew S. Mathers Scholarship
Deadline: September 1

Award Amount: $1,000

No. of scholarships: 1

Website:
https://andrewmatherslaw.com/andrew-s-mathers-scholarship/

Requirements:

- High school or college student
- Demonstrate financial need

Pizza Hut Foundation Scholarship
Deadline: September 7

Award Amount: $2,000 to $5,000

No. of scholarships: Varies

Website:
https://www.pizzahutfoundation.org/programs/

Requirements:

- Legal residents of the U.S., Guam, or D.C.
- At least age 17 and no older than 26
- Enrolled in or on track to apply to two- or four-year colleges, universities, vocational-technical schools, or trade schools
- Eligible for federal financial aid at the institution they plan to attend

Jones T-Shirts Scholarship

Deadline: September 10

Award Amount: $1,000

No. of scholarships: 1

Website: http://www.jonestshirts.com/scholarship

Requirements: Current student enrolled at a U.S. college or university

The Gates Scholarship

Deadline: September 15

Award Amount: Full college tuition for all four years

No. of scholarships: 300

Website:
https://www.thegatesscholarship.org/scholarship

Requirements:

- High school senior
- Ethnic minority (black, Hispanic or Asian)
- U.S. citizen, national, or permanent resident
- Plan to enroll full-time in a four-year degree program at a U.S. accredited, not-for-profit, private or public college or university
- Minimum 3.3 GPA
- Meet Federal Pell Grant eligibility criteria

Oracle Corporate Scholars/UNCF Program

Deadline:	September 20
Award Amount:	$10,000
No. of scholarships:	10
Website:	https://www.uncf.org

Requirements:

- U.S. citizen, national, or permanent resident
- African American, Native American, or Hispanic
- Must have attended a high school in the U.S.
- College sophomore, junior, or senior
- Minimum 3.0 GPA
- Majoring in applied mathematics, business, business-related, computer engineering, computer information systems, computer science, cyber security, information management systems, information technology, law, management information systems, marketing, mathematics, pre-law, product development, software development

Oracle Developer Scholars/UNCF Program
Deadline: September 20

Award Amount: $10,000

No. of scholarships: 25

Website: https://www.uncf.org

Requirements:

- U.S. citizen, national, or permanent resident
- African American, Native American, or Hispanic
- College sophomore or junior
- Minimum 3.0 GPA
- Majoring in computer engineering, computer science, software engineering

Apple HBCU Scholars Program
Deadline: September 22

Award Amount: $15,000 for senior year of study

No. of scholarships: Varies

Website:
https://www.tmcf.org/students-alumni/corp-scholar-programs/apple-hbcu-scholars/

Requirements:

- Undergraduate sophomore, junior, senior pursuing a fifth year of study, graduate student, or law school student
- Graduating between December 2024 and May 2026
- Enrolled full-time at a four-year accredited HBCU/PBI

- Willing and able to participate in a 12-week summer internship program
- Maintain good academic standing
- No disciplinary infractions on academic record
- Prior internship experience strongly preferred
- Prior leadership experience

Schwarzman Scholars Program

Deadline: September 22

Award Amount: $3,500 stipend, tuition, room and board, travel to/from Beijing, China, laptop, books and supplies

No. of scholarships: Up to 200 worldwide

Website:
https://www.schwarzmanscholars.org/admissions/

Requirements:

- Undergraduate degree completed by August 1
- Age between 18 and 28
- English language proficiency

Don't Text and Drive Scholarship

Deadline: September 30

Award Amount: $500 to $1,500

No. of scholarships: 2

Website:
http://www.digitalresponsibility.org/scholarships/

Requirements:

- U.S. citizen or legal resident
- High school student, undergraduate or graduate college student

Key Thinkers Scholarship

Deadline: September 30

Award Amount: $1,000

No. of scholarships: 1

Website: https://www.moneykey.com/scholarship/

Requirements:

- U.S. citizen or permanent resident
- 18 years or older
- Enrolled as a full-time student at an accredited college, university, or trade school in the U.S.
- Minimum 3.0 GPA

McGraw Law Group First Responders Scholarship

Deadline: September 30

Award Amount: $1,000

No. of scholarships: 1

Website:
https://mccrawlawgroup.com/first-responders-scholarship-2023/

Requirements:

- Student enrolled in a college, university, graduate school, or law school. GED holders planning to attend college during the upcoming semester are also eligible.
- Minimum 3.0 GPA

OCTOBER

Knowmad Digital Marketing Scholarship
Deadline: October 1

Award Amount: $500

No. of scholarships: 1

Website:
https://www.internationalscholarships.com/3166/Knowmad-Digital-Marketing-Scholarship

Requirements:

- Attend an accredited U.S.-based accredited university
- Undergraduate or graduate student
- Be enrolled in a business, marketing, or communication related degree program

AES Engineering Scholarship
Deadline: October 8

Award Amount: $500

No. of scholarships: 1

Website:
http://www.aesengineers.com/scholarships.htm

Requirements: High school senior, undergraduate or graduate student

Wellington Management HBCU Scholars Program
Deadline: October 8

Award Amount: Up to $5,000

No. of scholarships: 1

Website:
https://www.wellington.com/en/about-us/hbcu-scholarship-program

Requirements:

- U.S. legal resident, citizen, or eligible noncitizen under Federal Title IV regulations
  Enrolled full-time as a sophomore or junior at the undergraduate level
- Attending a Historically Black College or University (HBCU)
- Minimum 3.0 GPA
- Majoring in accounting, business, economics, finance, technology, liberal arts, or STEM (science, technology, engineering and mathematics)

Dr. Pepper Tuition Giveaway
Deadline: October 12

Award Amount: $2,500 to $100,000

No. of scholarships: 20

Website: https://www.drpeppertuition.com/

Requirements: Student between the ages of 18-24

Maineri Law Firm Higher Education Scholarship

Deadline: October 12

Award Amount: $1,000

No. of scholarships: 1

Website: https://www.mainerilaw.com/scholarship

Requirements:

- U.S. citizen or lawful permanent resident
- Currently enrolled in a college undergraduate program
- At least 17 years old
- Minimum 3.0 GPA
- Planning to pursue graduate degrees in one of the following fields: Communications, Education, Environmental Studies, Geography, Geology, History, Journalism, Language, Literature, Political Science, Psychology

Tourism Leadership Council Scholarship Program

Deadline: October 13

Award Amount: Up to $2,000

No. of scholarships: Varies

Website:
https://tourismleadershipcouncil.com/scholarship-application-form

Requirements:

- High school senior or college student enrolled in a college or technical school
- Interested in pursuing a career in the culinary, tourism, or hospitality industry
- Minimum 3.0 GPA

Amy Lowell Poetry Traveling Scholarship

Deadline: October 15

Award Amount: $66,500

No. of scholarships: 1

Website:
https://opportunitydesk.org/2022/10/13/amy-lowell-poetry-traveling-scholarship-2023-2024/

Requirements:

- U.S. citizen
- Poet of American birth who is able and willing to spend one year outside the continent of North America
- No age requirement and no requirement that applicants be enrolled in a university or other education program

Daniels Scholarship Program

Deadline: October 15

Award Amount: Four-year renewable annually; last-dollar scholarship that covers students costs for tuition and fees after other scholarships, grants, and work study have been accepted.

No. of scholarships: Varies

Website: https://www.danielsfund.org/scholarships

Requirements:

- U.S. citizen or permanent resident
- High school senior
- Residents of and graduating from a high school in Colorado, New Mexico, Utah and Wyoming only
- Minimum SAT Math score of 470 and Writing score of 450, or a minimum ACT score of 17 in each category
- Demonstrate financial need

College Jumpstart Scholarship
Deadline: October 17

Award Amount: $1,000

No. of scholarships: 1

Website: http://www.jumpstart-scholarship.net/

Requirements:

- U.S. citizen or legal resident
- High school sophomore, junior, senior, college student, or non-traditional student
- Attend or plan to attend an accredited 2-year, 4-year, or vocational/trade school in the U.S.
- Be committed to using education to better your life and that of your family and/or community

Omega Psi Phi Fraternity International High School Essay Contest
Deadline: October 20

Award Amount: $1,000 to $5,000

No. of scholarships: 4

Website:
https://www.oppf.org/international-high-school-essay-contest/

Requirements: College-bound high school senior

Michael Jackson/UNCF Scholarship
Deadline: October 27

Award Amount: Up to $4,000

No. of scholarships: Varies

Website: http://www.uncf.org

Requirements:

- U.S. citizen, national, or permanent resident
- Undergraduate or graduate college student
- Attending a UNCF-affiliated university (see website for list)
- Minimum 2.5 GPA
- Majoring in communication arts or social sciences

American Bullion Scholarship Program
Deadline: October 31

Award Amount: $1,000

No. of scholarships: 3

Website:
https://www.americanbullion.com/scholarship/

Requirements:

- U.S. citizen or legal resident
- Undergraduate student
- Enrolled at an accredited U.S. college or university

Coca-Cola Scholars Program

Deadline: October 31

Award Amount: $20,000

No. of scholarships: 250

Website:
http://www.coca-colascholarsfoundation.org/applicants/#programs

Requirements:

- U.S. citizen, national, permanent/temporary resident, refugee, asylee, Cuban-Haitian entrant, or humanitarian parolee
- High school senior (home-schooled student may also apply)
- Minimum 3.0 GPA

Karen Riley Porter Attorney at Law Good Works Scholarship

Deadline: October 31

Award Amount: $1,000

No. of scholarships: 1

Website:
https://www.virginia-criminallawyer.com/good-works-scholarship-2021/

Requirements:

- Incoming college freshmen, undergraduates, graduate and law school student
- Attending an accredited U.S. educational institution
- Minimum 3.0 GPA
- Must show a dedicated interest in community service and projects pertaining to criminal justice

Lincoln Financial/UNCF Scholars Program
Deadline: October 31

Award Amount: Up to $3,000

No. of scholarships: Varies

Website: https://www.uncf.org

Requirements:

- U.S. citizen, national, or legal permanent resident
- Enrolled at an HBCU
- Currently enrolled as a college junior or senior attending a four-year, accredited institution
- Minimum 2.7 GPA

Money Metals Exchange Scholarship Program
Deadline: October 31

Award Amount: $500 to $2,500

No. of scholarships: 7

Website:
https://www.moneymetals.com/scholarship

Requirements:

- High school senior, undergraduate or graduate student
- Interested in or majoring in economics (economics does *not* need to be the student's major)

National Security Agency/Stokes Educational Scholarship Program
Deadline: October 31

Award Amount: Up to $30,000 per year for tuition/fees and a year-round salary

No. of scholarships: Varies

Website:
https://federaljobs.net/blog/the-stokes-educational-scholarship-program-nsa/

Requirements:

- U.S. citizen
- High school senior at the time of application
- Minimum 3.0 GPA
- Minimum SAT of 1600 or ACT of 25
- Majoring in computer science or computer/electrical engineering
- Eligible to be granted a security clearance
- Upon college graduation, must work in your area of study for NSA for at least one-and-one-half times the length of study

NOVEMBER

Denny's Hungry for Education Scholarship
Deadline: November 1

Award Amount: $2,000

No. of scholarships: 5

Website: http://www.hacu.net/hacu/scholarships.asp

Requirements:

- Hispanic heritage student
- Full- or part-time undergraduate or graduate student
- Enrolled at two- or four-year HACU-member institution

- Minimum 2.5 GPA
- Reside in one of the following states: AZ, CA, CO, DC., FL, GA, IL, NC, NM, NV, NY, SC, TX, or WA

(The) Newburyport Studio Scholarship

Deadline:	November 1
Award Amount:	Roundtrip international airfare of up to $1,500 to any part of the world, a $1,000 Airbnb gift card for a place to stay, and a $500 Visa gift card for other expenses.
No. of scholarships:	1
Website:	https://thenbptstudio.com/scholarship

Requirements:

- U.S. citizen
- Female between 18 and 22 years of age
- Based in the New England region of the U.S.
- Have a valid passport with at least eight months left before expiration
- Have an intense desire to travel outside of comfort zone

Simeone Miller LLP Scholarship

Deadline:	November 1
Award Amount:	$1,000
No. of scholarships:	1

Website:
https://www.simeonemiller.com/scholarship/

Requirement:	Currently enrolled or accepted as an undergraduate or law student

Women's Independence Scholarship Program
Deadline: November 1

Award Amount: $500 to $2,000 per quarter or semester

No. of scholarships: Varies

Website:
https://wispinc.org/new-applicant-eligibility/

Requirements:

- Female survivor of intimate partner abuse
- U.S. citizen or permanent legal resident
- Be physically separated from abuser a minimum of one year but not more than seven
- Have applied to or been officially accepted into an accredited course of study at a U.S. institution
- Have sought services from a non-profit agency that provides services to survivors of intimate partner abuse for a minimum of six (6) consecutive months
- Demonstrate a critical need for financial assistance
- Exhibit a strong desire and the ability to complete a training and/or academic program

Chick-Fil-A Community Scholarship Program
Deadline: November 1

Award Amount: $25,000

No. of scholarships: 12

Website:
https://www.chick-fil-a.com/communityscholars

Requirements:

- Resident of the United States, Puerto Rico or Canada
- Minimum 3.0 GPA
- Demonstrate financial need

- Recommended by a teacher, coach, or community leader
- Postsecondary undergraduate or graduate student or intend to enroll in undergraduate or graduate study for the upcoming academic year

Generation Google Scholarship

Deadline: November 15

Award Amount: $10,000

No. of scholarships: Varies

Website:
https://www.google.com/edu/scholarships/the-generation-google-scholarship/

Requirements:

- Ethnic minority (black, Hispanic, American Indian) OR female
- High school senior or currently enrolled as an undergraduate or graduate student
- Plan to be enrolled as a full-time student at a university in the U.S. in the upcoming academic year
- Pursuing a computer science or computer engineering degree, or a degree in a closely related technical field
- Exemplify leadership and a passion for technology
- Exhibit a strong record of academic achievement

Helmer, Conley & Kasselman Annual College Scholarship

Deadline: November 15

Award Amount: $500

No. of scholarships: 1

Website:
https://www.helmerlegal.com/college-scholarship/

Requirements:

- High school senior or current college student
- Enrolling in or currently enrolled in a two- or four-year college or university
- Intent to pursue a degree in law leading to bar eligibility and a license to practice law

Medical Library Association Scholarship
Deadline: November 15

Award Amount: $5,000

No. of scholarships: 1

Website: https://www.mlanet.org/p/cm/ld/fid=303

Requirements:

- U.S. or Canadian citizen or permanent resident
- Entering a master's program at an American Library Association-accredited graduate library school or, at the time of scholarship award, have completed no more than one-half of academic requirements of the graduate program

Jack Kent Cooke Foundation Scholarship
Deadline: November 17

Award Amount: Up to $40,000/year for 4 years

No. of scholarships: 40

Website:
http://www.jkcf.org/scholarship-programs/college-scholarship/

Requirements:

- High school senior
- Planning to enroll at an accredited four-year college or university for the upcoming fall
- Minimum 3.5 GPA
- Minimum SAT combined critical reading and math score of 1200+ and/or ACT composite score of 26+
- Demonstrate financial need

ServiceScape Scholarship

Deadline: November 29

Award Amount: $1,000

No. of scholarships: 1

Website: https://www.servicescape.com/scholarship

Requirements:

- At least 18 years old
- Attending or plan to attend an accredited college, university or trade school

Bachus & Schanker, LLC Scholarship

Deadline: November 30

Award Amount: $2,000

No. of scholarships: 1

Website: http://www.coloradolaw.net/scholarship/

Requirements:

- High school senior or undergraduate student
- Accepted to or attending a four-year university
- Minimum 3.0 GPA

Driver Education Initiative Scholarship
Deadline: November 30

Award Amount: $1,000

No. of scholarships: 1

Website: http://www.dmvedu.org/scholarship/

Requirements:

- High school sophomore, junior, senior, or college freshman
- Enrolled as a full-time student

Education Matters Scholarship
Deadline: November 30

Award Amount: $5,000

No. of scholarships: 1

Website:
https://www.unigo.com/scholarships/our-scholarships/education-matters-scholarship

Requirements:

- Legal resident of the U.S. or the District of Columbia
- Age 13 or older
- Currently enrolled in an accredited post-secondary institution of higher education

(The) John Galt Scholarship for Future Supply Chain Leaders

Deadline: November 30

Award Amount: $10,000

No. of scholarships: 1

Website: https://johngalt.com/scholarship/

Requirements:

- Enrolled as a student at an accredited higher education institution in the U.S. for the current academic year
- Enrolled full-time in a supply management or S&OP with the intention of seeking a career in the supply chain field
- Demonstrate financial need
- Constantly seeking opportunities to further develop skills and character

Kopfler & Hermann Overcoming Adversity Scholarship

Deadline: November 30

Award Amount: $1,000

No. of scholarships: 1

Website:
https://kopflerhermann.com/2021-overcoming-adversity-scholarship/

Requirements:

- Enrolled in college, graduate school, or be a GED holder who is about to attend college
- Minimum 3.0 GPA
- Demonstrate that although student has encountered hardship, they have persevered and committed to success

Semper Solaris Scholarship
Deadline: November 30

Award Amount: $500 to $3,000

No. of scholarships: 4

Website:
https://www.sempersolaris.com/semper-cares-initiative/scholarships/

Requirements:

- Current college freshman, sophomore, junior, senior, graduate student, or attending a military academy
- Enrolled full-time at an accredited college or university
- Minimum 3.0 GPA

DECEMBER

Dell Scholars Program
Deadline: December 1

Award Amount: $20,000 over the course of six years

No. of scholarships: 300

Website: http://www.dellscholars.org

Requirements:

- Participating in a Michael & Susan Dell Foundation approved readiness program in grades 11 and 12 (e.g., IDEA Academy, GEAR UP, Kipp Academy and Upward Bound)
- High school senior graduating from an accredited high school
- Planning to enroll full-time in a bachelor's degree program at an accredited college/university
- Minimum 2.4 GPA
- Demonstrate need for financial assistance
- Eligible to receive federal student aid

Hagan Scholarship

Deadline: December 1

Award Amount: $6,000 (Renewable)

No. of scholarships: Varies

Website: https://haganscholarships.org/

Requirements:

- U.S. citizen
- High school senior
- Attending an eligible public high school
- Minimum 3.75 GPA
- Enrolled or planning to enroll at an eligible four-year college or university the first semester following high school graduation
- Must work 240 hours prior to fall semester college enrollment
- Must apply for federal and state grants, if eligible
- Must not have a felony conviction

Herrman & Herrman Innovation Scholarship
Deadline: December 1

Award Amount: $1,000 to $2,500

No. of scholarships: 3

Website:
https://www.herrmanandherrman.com/scholarship/

Requirements:

- High school junior or senior, or undergraduate student
- Undergraduate students must be enrolled at a Texas-based two- to four-year college or university

Kuru Footwear Scholarship
Deadline: December 1

Award Amount: $1,000

No. of scholarships: 1

Website:
https://www.kurufootwear.com/scholarship

Requirements:

- U.S. citizen
- Incoming freshman, college sophomore, junior, or senior
- Enrolled full-time at an accredited college or university
- Minimum 2.5 GPA

Lamber-Goodnow Injury Law Team Education Scholarships

Deadline: December 1

Award Amount: $1,000

No. of scholarships: 8

Website:
https://lambergoodnow.com/scholarships/

Requirements:

- Enrolled at an accredited high school, college or university, including four-year, community colleges and junior colleges
- Minimum 2.8 GPA

Overseas Press Club Foundation Scholarship

Deadline: December 1

Award Amount: $3,000 to $4,000

No. of scholarships: 16

Website:
https://overseaspressclubfoundation.org/apply.html

Requirements:

- Undergraduate or graduate student studying at an American college or university, OR American student studying abroad
- Aspiring to become a foreign correspondent

Ron Brown Scholar Program
Deadline: December 1

Award Amount: $40,000 ($10,000 each year for four years)

No. of scholarships: 10 to 20

Website: http://www.ronbrown.org

Requirements:

- African American
- U.S. citizen or permanent resident
- Current high school senior
- Demonstrate financial need
- Demonstrate academic achievement
- Exhibit leadership ability
- Participate in community service activities

MetLife Foundation/UNCF Scholarship
Deadline: December 2

Award Amount: $7,333 (renewable for one year)

No. of scholarships: Varies

Website: https://www.uncf.org

Requirements:

- African-American student
- U.S. citizen, national, or permanent resident
- College junior
- Enrolled at an accredited HBCU
- Minimum 3.0 GPA
- Majoring in business, finance, or accounting
- Demonstrate financial need

National Space Club and Foundation Scholarship
Deadline: December 4

Award Amount: $10,000

No. of scholarships: 1

Website:
https://www.spaceclub.org/scholarship/index.html

Requirements:

- U.S. citizen
- High school senior, undergraduate, or graduate student
- Plan to pursue a career in the STEM fields
- Plan to attend an accredited U.S. college or university to follow a course of study to pursue a career in a STEM field, with a preference for those with space-related interests

PixelPlex STEM Scholarship
Deadline: December 5

Award Amount: $2,000

No. of scholarships: 1

Website: https://pixelplex.io/scholarship/

Requirements:

- U.S. citizen or permanent resident
- Enrolled or accepted in a college or university in the U.S.
- Field of study is related to science, technology, engineering, math, economics, or business

Hennessy Fellows/TMCF Scholarship
Deadline: December 6

Award Amount: $20,000/academic year for up to two years plus a one-time $10,000 stipend

No. of scholarships: Varies

Website:
https://www.tmcf.org/students-alumni/corp-scholar-programs/hennessy-fellows/

Requirements:

- Age 21+ at the time of application
- Enrolled in the first year in an HBCU graduate program
- Minimum 3.25 GPA

R&D Systems Scholarship
Deadline: December 8

Award Amount: $1,500

No. of scholarships: 1

Website:
https://www.rndsystems.com/grants-scholarships/scholarship-application

Requirements:

- Student studying in a college/university within the U.S., Canada, and European countries only
- Enrolled or accepted for enrollment at the time of application
- Declared major in a science-related field (e.g., life science, medical science, health science, nursing, biology, chemistry, environmental sciences, medical engineering)

Generation Google Women in Gaming Scholarship

Deadline: December 10

Award Amount: $10,000

No. of scholarships: Varies

Website:
https://buildyourfuture.withgoogle.com/scholarships/generation-google-scholarship/

Requirements:

- Female college students
- Intend to be enrolled in or accepted as a full-time student in a bachelor's, master's, or PhD program
- Attending an accredited college or university in the United States or Canada
- Be studying video game programming, game engineering, game design and development, or a closely related technical field in gaming
- Demonstrate a strong academic record
- Demonstrate financial need
- Exemplify leadership and demonstrate passion for increasing the involvement of women in gaming

UNCF Social Justice Scholarship
Deadline: December 14

Award Amount: Up to $5,000

No. of scholarships: 10

Website: https://www.uncf.org

Requirements:

- U.S. citizen, national or permanent resident
- African-American student
- College junior or senior
- Attending an HBCU
- Majoring in criminal justice, political science, prelaw, forensic science, or criminology
- Minimum 2.5 GPA
- Permanent resident of Connecticut, Vermont, New York, or New Jersey

Attorney Ronald D. Weiss College Scholarship
Deadline: December 15

Award Amount: $2,500

No. of scholarships: 1

Website:
https://www.ny-bankruptcy.com/scholarship/

Requirements:

- Currently enrolled in a college or university or planning to enroll as a freshman for the upcoming academic year
- Be in good academic standing with current educational institution
- If under 18, permission from parent or guardian is required

Burger King Scholars
Deadline: December 15

Award Amount: $12,500 per academic year for up to four years

No. of scholarships: 2,000

Website: http://www.bkmclamorefoundation.org

Requirements:

- Resident of U.S., Canada or Puerto Rico
- Graduating high school senior only
- Planned enrollment in accredited two- or four-year college in fall
- Minimum 2.5 GPA

Creative Safety Supply Scholarship
Deadline: December 15

Award Amount: $1,000

No. of scholarships: 1

Website:
https://www.creativesafetysupply.com/scholarship/

Requirements:

- U.S. citizen or permanent resident
- Enrolled in a college, university, or vocational school for the upcoming term
- Minimum 3.0 GPA

Foreclosure.com Scholarship

Deadline:	December 15
Award Amount:	First place - $4,000; Second and Third Place - $1,000 each
No. of scholarships:	3
Website:	http://www.foreclosure.com/scholarship
Requirements:	Currently enrolled undergraduate college students (graduate students, law students and/or high school seniors are *not* eligible)

Law Offices of Daniel Kim Scholarship

Deadline:	December 15
Award Amount:	$5,000
No. of scholarships:	1

Website:
https://usaccidentlawyer.com/the-law-offices-of-daniel-kim-scholarship/

Requirements:

- U.S. citizen
- Currently enrolled or accepted to a university/college
- Must be in good academic standing with current educational institution
- Minimum 3.0 GPA

Sachs Marketing Group General Marketing Education Scholarship

Deadline: December 15

Award Amount: $1,000

No. of scholarships: 1

Website:
https://sachsmarketinggroup.com/general-marketing-education-scholarship-marketing-education/

Requirement: Any student currently enrolled in any accredited college

(The) Takeoff Scholarship Program

Deadline: December 15

Award Amount: $10,000

No. of scholarships: 2

Website:
https://takeoffscholarship.org/#education-soul-call-to-action

Requirements:

- Black or African American; American Indian or Alaska Native; or Hispanic or Latino
- Enrolled or planning to enroll in full-time undergraduate study at an accredited four-year college/university for the upcoming academic year
- Attending a college/university in one of the following states: Alabama, Georgia, North Carolina, South Carolina, or Tennessee
- Be a current college undergraduate having completed at least 24 credits at the time of application
- Pursuing a degree and career in one of the following areas: architecture, building science, civil engineering, construction management or construction engineering, entrepreneurship (with building supply, construction trade, or homebuilding focus), finance (with a real estate focus), real estate

Equitable Excellence Scholarship Program

Deadline: December 16

Award Amount: $2,500 to $25,000

No. of scholarships: 369

Website:
https://learnmore.scholarsapply.org/equitableexcellence/

Requirements:

- U.S. citizen of legal resident
- Current high school senior residing in the U.S. or Puerto Rico

- Plan to enroll full-time in an accredited two-year or four-year college or university in the U.S. in the upcoming fall semester
- Be willing to provide a release to publicize their identities and information about their achievements along with photographs for use in program promotion

Anheuser-Busch Foundation/UNCF Scholarship

Deadline: December 29

Award Amount: $2,500

No. of scholarships: Varies

Website: https://www.uncf.org

Requirements:

- Graduating senior enrolled at any UNCF-member institution
- Minimum 2.5 GPA
- Majoring in business, chemical engineering, electrical engineering, industrial engineering, mechanical engineering, or supply chain management and logistics
- Demonstrate unmet financial need

Frank L. Greathouse Government Accounting Scholarship

Deadline: December 30

Award Amount: $10,000

No. of scholarships: 2

Website:
https://www.gfoa.org/available-scholarships

Requirements:

- Citizen or permanent resident of the U.S. or Canada
- Plan to pursue a career in state/provincial or local government finance
- Enrolled full-time as an upper level undergraduate or graduate student
- Majoring in accounting

Goldberg-Miller Public Finance Scholarship

Deadline: December 30

Award Amount: $25,000

No. of scholarships: 1

Website:
https://www.gfoa.org/available-scholarships

Requirements:

- Citizen or permanent resident of the U.S. or Canada
- Plan to pursue a career in state/provincial or local government finance
- Enrolled full-time as a graduate student
- Majoring in course of study related to state/local government finance

Government Finance Professional Development Scholarship

Deadline: December 30

Award Amount: $10,000

No. of scholarships: 4

Website:
https://www.gfoa.org/about-gfoa/student-opportunities/gfoa-scholarships-full-and-part-time-students

Requirements:

- Citizen or permanent resident of the U.S. or Canada
- Plan to pursue a career in state/provincial or local government finance
- Enrolled part-time as a graduate student
- Majoring in public administration, (governmental) accounting, finance, economics, or business administration (with specific focus on government)
- Employed at least two years by one or more state or local governments

Minorities in Government Finance Scholarship
Deadline: December 30

Award Amount: $10,000

No. of scholarships: 1

Website:
https://www.gfoa.org/about-gfoa/student-opportunities/gfoa-scholarships-full-and-part-time-students

Requirements:

- Citizen or permanent resident of the U.S. or Canada
- Plan to pursue a career in state/provincial or local government finance

- Enrolled full-time or part-time as an upper level undergraduate or graduate student
- Majoring in public administration, (governmental) accounting, finance, economics, or business administration (with specific focus on government)

Achieve Today Scholarship Fund
Deadline: December 31

Award Amount: $1,000

No. of scholarships: 1

Website:
http://www.achievetoday.com/scholarships

Requirements: Current student at an accredited U.S. college or university

CC Bank's Young Scholars Scholarship
Deadline: December 31

Award Amount: $2,000

No. of scholarships: 5

Website: https://ccbank.us/scholarship/

Requirements:

- U.S. resident
- Under the age of 30
- Minimum 3.0 GPA
- Enrolled in an academic institution

DM Cantor College or Law Student Scholarship
Deadline: December 31

Award Amount: $2,500

No. of scholarships: 1

Website:
https://dmcantor.com/criminal-defense-lawyer-scholarship-fund

Requirements:

- Age 18 years or older
- Currently attending or planning to attend an accredited, U.S.-based college, university, or law school

Driven Coffee Scholarship
Deadline: December 31

Award Amount: $100 to $500

No. of scholarships: 3

Website:
https://www.drivencoffee.com/scholarship/

Requirement: Enrolled full-time at a college or university within the U.S. or Canada

Gen and Kelly Tanabe Scholarship
Deadline: December 31

Award Amount: $1,000

No. of scholarships: 3

Website: http://www.genkellyscholarship.com

Requirements:

- U.S. citizen or legal resident
- High school student from 9th to 12th grade OR undergraduate or graduate college student

HeadsetPlus.com Annual College Scholarship

Deadline: December 31

Award Amount: $1,000

No. of scholarships: 1

Website:
http://headsetplus.com/newsdesk95/newsdesk_info.html

Requirements:

- U.S. citizen
- Age 16 or older
- High school senior entering college, current college students or graduate students
- Minimum 3.0 GPA

iVein Health & Wellness Scholarship

Deadline: December 31

Award Amount: $2,500

No. of scholarships: 1

Website: https://www.ivein.com/scholarship/

Requirements:

- Current full-time undergraduate/graduate student
- Attending an accredited U.S. university or college
- Minimum 3.7 GPA

LawnStarter Lawntrepreneur Scholarship

Deadline: December 31

Award Amount: $1,000

No. of scholarships: 1

Website: https://www.lawnstarter.com/scholarship

Requirements:

- High school senior or full time college student enrolled in a two-year, four-year, or graduate program
- Currently own a lawn care business, ran a lawn care business in the past, OR plan on starting a business of any kind upon graduating college
- Have the willpower, work ethic, and desire to build the next great business

Mattress Fun Yearly Scholarship

Deadline: December 31

Award Amount: $1,000

No. of scholarships: 1

Website:
http://www.handsonmattress.com/best-mattress-yearly-scholarship/

Requirements:

- Current high school (or home-schooled) senior attending school in the United States OR current college student already studying at an accredited U.S. post-secondary institution
- Minimum 3.0 GPA

Nelson Cabinetry Scholarship
Deadline: December 31

Award Amount: $1,500

No. of scholarships: 3

Website: https://nelsonkb.com/scholarships

Requirements:

- Legal U.S. resident or citizen
- Enrolled in an accredited high school, college, or university within the U.S.
- High school students must be entering or finishing their senior year in order to be eligible.
- College students must be enrolled at an accredited school for at least one full calendar year to be eligible.

Sieben Edmunds Miller Criminal Justice Scholarship
Deadline: December 31

Award Amount: $1,000

No. of scholarships: 1

Website:
https://siebenedmunds.com/law-scholarship/

Requirements:

- Undergraduate or law school college student
- Pursuing a career as a criminal defense attorney
- Demonstrate financial need

Society for Technical Communication Scholarship
Deadline: December 31

Award Amount: $500

No. of scholarships: 1

Website: https://www.stc.org/scholarship/

Requirements:

- Completed at least one year of post-secondary education
- Working toward a bachelor's degree, graduate degree, or a graduate certificate in communication of information about technical subjects
- Have at least one full year of academic work remaining to complete degree program

JANUARY

AutoTransport.com Scholarship
Deadline: January 1

Award Amount: $500 to $1,000

No. of scholarships: 3

Website:
https://autotransport.com/auto-transport-scholarship/

Requirements:

- Student enrolled at a college or university
- Interest in automotive technology and/or logistics

John Lennon Endowed/UNCF Scholarship
Deadline: January 4

Award Amount: Up to $5,000

No. of scholarships: Varies

Website: https://www.uncf.org

Requirements:

- U.S. citizen, national or permanent resident
- Attending a UNCF-member affiliated HBCU
- Full-time college undergraduate student
- Majoring in communications, mass communications, mass media arts, music, performing arts
- Minimum 3.0 GPA

MarvelOptics National Scholarship Contest
Deadline: January 5

Award Amount: $1,500

No. of scholarships: 2

Website:
https://marveloptics.com/blog/scholarship-program/

Requirements:

- Current, full-time undergraduate student
- Attending an accredited two-year or four-year American college or university

Switzer Environmental Fellowship

Deadline: January 8

Award Amount: $15,000

No. of scholarships: Varies

Website:
https://www.switzernetwork.org/become-fellow

Requirements:

- U.S. citizen
- Full-time graduate student enrolled in environmental-related course study
- Attending an accredited graduate institute in one of the following states: CA, CT, MA, ME, NH, RI or VT
- Very strong academic qualifications

Asian & Pacific Islander American Scholarship Fund

Deadline: January 9

Award Amount: $2,500 to $20,000

No. of scholarships: Varies

Website:
http://www.apiasf.org/scholarship_apiasf.html

Requirements:

- Asian and/or Pacific Islander ethnicity as defined by the U.S. Census
- U.S. citizen or legal resident
- Enrolling as an undergraduate student in a U.S. accredited college or university in the fall of the upcoming academic year

- Submit FAFSA by April
- Minimum 2.7 GPA

Future Leaders in Technology Scholarship

Deadline: January 9

Award Amount: $2,500 (college students)
$1,000 (high school seniors)

No. of scholarships: 2

Website: https://virtasant.com/scholarship/

Requirements:

- Female or minority student
- High school senior or college/university student
- Attending a four-year accredited institution, 2-year college, vocational school, technical school, or be a high school student planning to attend one of the above
- Pursuing a degree in computer science, engineering, mathematics, or other material sciences
- Minimum 3.5 GPA

(The) Jackie Robinson Foundation Scholarship

Deadline: January 10

Award Amount: $7,500 per year for up to four years

No. of scholarships: Varies

Website: http://www.jackierobinson.org

Requirements:

- U.S. citizen
- Minority high school senior
- Enrollment at an accredited four-year college/university within the U.S.
- Demonstrate a record of academic excellence
- Demonstrate financial need
- Demonstrate leadership potential and a dedication to community service

Jones T-Shirts Scholarship

Deadline: January 10

Award Amount: $1,000

No. of scholarships: 1

Website: http://www.jonestshirts.com/scholarship

Requirements: Current student enrolled at a U.S. college or university

Fidelity Scholars Program

Deadline: January 11

Award Amount: Varies

No. of scholarships: Varies

Website: https://www.uncf.org

Requirements:

- Historically underserved or underrepresented student (e.g., Black, Latino, Native American, Asian American/Pacific Islander)
- Ages 16 to 24

- Permanent resident of FL, MA, NM, NJ, NC, TX or Washington, DC
- Minimum 2.5 GPA
- Pell Grant eligible and/or demonstrate financial need
- Attending college as an incoming freshman in the fall semester at a four-year accredited college or university in the state in which you reside

Carson Scholars Program

Deadline: January 12

Award Amount: $1,000

No. of scholarships: Varies

Website: https://carsonscholars.org/scholarships/

Requirements:

- Grades 4 to 11
- Attend an accredited K-12 school in the U.S.
- Nominated by current educator
- Minimum 3.75 GPA
- Display humanitarian qualities through community service

Irene S. Wischer Educational Foundation Scholarship

Deadline: January 12

Award Amount: Up to $10,800 per year

No. of scholarships: Varies

Website:
https://www.frostbank.com/Pages/wischer-scholarship.aspx

Requirements:

- U.S. citizen
- Legal resident of Texas for 12 consecutive months prior to application submission
- Demonstrate good character; preference will be given to "applicants who are Christians and attend church regularly"
- Demonstrate academic ability
- Demonstrate financial need

John F. Kennedy Profile in Courage Scholarship

Deadline: January 12

Award Amount: First Place - $10,000
Second Place - $1,000
Third Place - $500 (five finalists)

No. of scholarships: 7

Website:
http://www.jfklibrary.org/Education/Profile-in-Courage-Essay-Contest.aspx

Requirements:

- U.S. citizen
- High school student grade nine through twelve attending public, private, parochial, or home schools; OR
- Under the age of twenty enrolled in a high school correspondence/GED program in any of the 50 states, the District of Columbia, or the U.S. territories; or attending school overseas

Frederick Douglass Bicentennial/UNCF Scholarship
Deadline: January 13

Award Amount: Up to $10,000

No. of scholarships: 2

Website: https://www.uncf.org

Requirements:

- U. S. citizen, U.S. national or permanent resident
- Enrolled full-time as a rising senior or 5th year senior at any accredited public or private four-year HBCU
- Minimum 3.5 GPA
- Demonstrate a commitment to community service
- Demonstrate unmet financial need

Washington Crossing Foundation Scholarship
Deadline: January 15

Award Amount: $500 to $5,000

No. of scholarships: Varies

Website: https://www.gwcf.org/scholarship

Requirements:

- U.S. citizen
- High school senior
- Planning career in local, state or federal government service

National Press Photographers Foundation
Deadline: January 16

Award Amount: $2,000

No. of scholarships: 14

Website: https://nppf.org/scholarship-competition/

Requirements:

- Undergraduate or graduate student enrolled at a four-year program at a U.S. college or university. Foreign students are eligible.
- Students in two-year programs may apply only if they are enrolled in a fall semester four-year program

Catherine W. Pierce/UNCF Scholarship

Deadline: January 18

Award Amount: $3,400

No. of scholarships: Varies

Website: https://www.uncf.org

Requirements:

- College student enrolled full-time at any U.S. accredited four-year institution
- Minimum 2.5 GPA
- Pursuing a degree in art, art history, or art studies

Chevron/UNCF Corporate Scholars Program

Deadline: January 18

Award Amount: Up to $15,000 (two-year renewable at $7,500)

No. of scholarships: Varies

Website: https://www.uncf.org

Requirements:

- U.S. citizen, national, or permanent resident
- African-American, Native American, Alaska Native, Asian Pacific Islander American, Hispanic American
- High school senior
- Enrolling in fall semester as a full-time, first-year student at an accredited U.S. four-year college or university
- Minimum 3.0 GPA
- Display interest in majoring in computer science or engineering
- Planning to attend college in or have a permanent address in the following states: Texas, Louisiana, Mississippi, or California
- Demonstrate financial need

Budweiser Natalie Johnson/UNCF Scholarship and Internship Program

Deadline:	January 29
Award Amount:	$6,500
No. of scholarships:	Varies
Website:	https://www.uncf.org

Requirements:

- College sophomore or junior
- Attending a four-year, accredited HBCU
- Minimum 2.8 GPA
- Majoring in chemical engineering, chemistry, electrical engineering, industrial engineering, mechanical engineering, supply chain management and logistics

Technology Addiction Awareness Scholarship

Deadline: January 30

Award Amount: $500 to $1,500

No. of scholarships: 2

Website:
http://www.digitalresponsibility.org/scholarships/

Requirements:

- U.S. citizen or legal resident
- High school student, undergraduate or graduate college student

ACIS Travel Is Education Scholarship

Deadline: January 31

Award Amount: $500 to $1,000

No. of scholarships: 4

Website: http://www.acis.com/students/scholarships

Requirements:

- Student in grades 6 through 12
- Have traveled on an ACIS tour in the past year

Advocates Law Scholarship

Deadline: January 31

Award Amount: $1,000

No. of scholarships: 1

Website:
https://www.advocateslaw.com/scholarship/

Requirement: Student enrolled at an accredited educational institution in the U.S.

Arthur Lockwood Beneventi Law Scholarship
Deadline: January 31

Award Amount: $2,000

No. of scholarships: 1

Website:
https://www.dar.org/national-society/scholarships

Requirements:

- U.S. citizen
- Attending an accredited U.S. law school
- Minimum 3.25 GPA

Edward G. and Helen A. Borgens Elementary and Secondary Teacher Education Scholarship
Deadline: January 31

Award Amount: Up to $1,500

No. of scholarships: 2

Website:
https://www.dar.org/national-society/scholarships

Requirements:

- U.S. citizen
- Age 25 or older
- Attending an accredited U.S. college or university
- Minimum 3.25 GPA

Houston Livestock Show and Rodeo Scholarship
Deadline: January 31

Award Amount: Up to $4,000 per semester

No. of scholarships: 800

Website:
https://www.rodeohouston.com/Educational-Support/Scholarships/Apply

Requirements:

- U.S. citizen AND Texas resident
- Graduating high school senior from eligible school
- Plan to attend an accredited, not-for-profit university in the state of Texas
- Submit the FAFSA for the current year

I Have a Dream Scholarship
Deadline: January 31

Award Amount: $1,500

No. of scholarships: 1

Website:
https://www.unigo.com/scholarships/our-scholarships/i-have-a-dream-scholarship

Requirements:

- Age 13 or older
- Legal U.S. resident
- Currently enrolled in an accredited post-secondary institution of higher education, or enrolled no later than the fall of 2023

Leo W. and Alberta V. Thomas Utz Scholarship
Deadline: January 31

Award Amount: $4,000

No. of scholarships: 3

Website:
https://www.dar.org/national-society/scholarships

Requirements:

- U.S. citizen
- Attending an accredited U.S. college or university
- Minimum 3.25 GPA

Mary Elizabeth Lockwood Beneventi MBA Scholarship
Deadline: January 31

Award Amount: $2,000

No. of scholarships: 1

Website:
https://www.dar.org/national-society/scholarships

Requirements:

- U.S. citizen
- Graduate student majoring in business administration
- Attending an accredited U.S. college or university
- Minimum 3.25 GPA

Michael T. and Mary L. Cloyd Scholarship
Deadline: January 31

Award Amount: $3,000

No. of scholarships: 2

Website:
https://www.dar.org/national-society/scholarships

Requirements:

- U.S. citizen
- Attending an accredited U.S. college or university
- Undergraduate in junior year
- Studying in the field of archives management with a preference for students specializing in American history
- Minimum 3.0 GPA

Nellie Love Butcher Music Scholarship

Deadline: January 31

Award Amount: $5,000

No. of scholarships: 1

Website:
https://www.dar.org/national-society/scholarships

Requirements:

- U.S. citizen
- High school senior
- Pursuing an education in piano or voice
- Special consideration given to students currently attending the Duke Ellington School of the Performing Arts in Washington, DC
- Minimum 3.0 GPA

PlayStation Career Pathways Program
Deadline: January 31

Award Amount: Up to $10,000

No. of scholarships: Varies

Website: https://www.uncf.org

Requirements:

- U.S. citizen, national, or permanent resident
- African-American student
- College freshman attending an HBCU, UNCF-affiliated, or four-year college
- Minimum 3.0 GPA
- Majoring in computer and information sciences, computer engineering, engineering, or computer science

Return2College Scholarship
Deadline: January 31

Award Amount: $1,000

No. of scholarships: 1

Website:
http://www.return2college.com/awardprogram.cfm

Requirements:

- U.S. citizen or legal resident
- Age 17 or older; no maximum age limit
- Plan to enroll or be enrolled full or part time at a college or university within 12 months after scholarship award

Richard and Elizabeth Dean Scholarship
Deadline: January 31

Award Amount: $5,000

No. of scholarships: 2

Website: https://www.dar.org/general-scholarship

Requirements:

- U.S. citizen
- High school senior
- Attending an accredited U.S. college or university
- Minimum 4.0 GPA

Robert Hunter Swadley Horticulture Scholarship
Deadline: January 31

Award Amount: Varies

No. of scholarships: 2

Website:
https://www.dar.org/national-society/scholarships

Requirements:

- U.S. citizen
- High school senior
- Resident of California
- Attending an accredited U.S. college or university
- Majoring in horticulture
- Minimum 3.0 GPA

Spencer Educational Foundation Full-Time Master's Scholarship

Deadline: January 31

Award Amount: $10,000

No. of scholarships: Varies

Website: https://www.spencered.org/scholarships

Requirements:

- Enrolled full-time as a graduate student in a master's program
- Attending an accredited college/university in the U.S. or Canada for the upcoming academic year
- Majoring or minoring in risk management/insurance, or a related field of study
- Seeking a career in risk management/insurance
- Minimum 3.3 GPA

Spencer Educational Foundation Part-Time Master's Scholarship

Deadline: January 31

Award Amount: Varies

No. of scholarships: Varies

Website: https://www.spencered.org/scholarships

Requirements:

- Enrolled online or part-time (12 hours or more per year) as a graduate student in a master's program
- Attending an accredited college/university in the U.S. or Canada for the upcoming academic year

- Studying risk management/insurance, or a related field of study
- Seeking a career in risk management/insurance and/or actuarial science
- Minimum 3.3 GPA
- Provide documentation outlining employer's tuition reimbursement policy

Spencer Educational Foundation Undergraduate Scholarship

Deadline: January 31

Award Amount: From $5,000 to $10,000

No. of scholarships: Varies

Website: https://www.spencered.org/scholarships

Requirements:

- Enrolled full-time as an undergraduate student
- Attending an accredited college/university in the U.S. or Canada for the upcoming academic year
- Majoring or minoring in risk management/insurance, or a related field of study
- Seeking a career in risk management/insurance
- Minimum 3.3 GPA

William Robert Findley Graduate Chemistry Scholarship

Deadline: January 31

Award Amount: $2,000

No. of scholarships: 1

Website: https://www.dar.org/general-scholarship

Requirements:

- U.S. citizen
- Full-time graduate student
- Attending an accredited U.S. college or university
- Majoring in chemistry
- Minimum 3.25 GPA

FEBRUARY

Harry S. Truman Scholarship Foundation

Deadline:	First Tuesday in February
Award Amount:	Covers most costs for graduate school including tuition, fees, room and board, and books
No. of scholarships:	55 to 65

Website:
https://www.truman.gov/candidates/faq-candidates/

Requirements:

- U.S. citizen
- Graduate or doctoral student planning to enroll in next four years (deferrals are allowed)
- Extensive record of campus and community service
- Commitment to a career in government or the nonprofit and advocacy sectors
- Communication skills and a high probability of becoming a "change agent"
- Strong academic record with likely acceptance to the graduate school of the candidate's choice

Aspiring Writers/Go On Girl Book Club Scholarship
Deadline: February 1

Award Amount: $1,000

No. of scholarships: 1

Website:
https://goongirl.org/scholarships/aspiring-writer

Requirements:

- U.S. citizen or resident alien
- Strong connection to identify with the African Diaspora
- Full-time student at an HBCU
- Minimum 2.5 GPA

Epsilon Sigma Alpha Foundation
Deadline: February 1

Award Amount: $550 to $7,500

No. of scholarships: Varies

Website:
http://www.epsilonsigmaalpha.org/scholarships-and-grants/scholarships

Requirements:

- Minimum 3.0 GPA OR a minimum SAT of 1030 or ACT of 22
- The Foundation has a number of various endowments with their own separate criteria

Ethnic Minority and Women's Enhancement Postgraduate Scholarship

Deadline: February 1

Award Amount: $10,000

No. of scholarships: 26

Website:
http://www.ncaa.org/ethnic-minority-and-women-s-enhancement-graduate-scholarship

Requirements:

- Ethnic minority or female undergraduate student
- At least in final season of NCAA athletics eligibility or will not be using any remaining athletics eligibility
- Seeking admission or have been accepted into a sports administration or other graduate program that will assist the applicant in obtaining a career in intercollegiate athletics
- Have not begun any initial postgraduate studies or graduate level hours
- Planning to enroll in an NCAA-member institution on a full-time basis
- Minimum 3.2 GPA

Ford Fund Scholarship

Deadline: February 1

Award Amount: $5,000

No. of scholarships: 17

Website:
https://www.hacu.net/hacu/scholarships.asp

Requirements:

- Attend a two-year or four-year Hispanic Association of Colleges and Universities (HACU) member institution
- Enrolled part-time or full-time as an undergraduate or graduate student
- Minimum 2.5 GPA
- Majoring in one of the following disciplines: Engineering: electrical, mechanical, chemical, manufacturing, process, quality, software, environmental, computer, robotics, systems, battery, automation controls, industrial, safety, materials, mechatronics; Math and Science; Urban and Regional Planning; Automotive/Manufacturing skilled trades

Landscape Architecture Foundation Diversity, Equity, and Inclusion Scholarship

Deadline: February 1

Award Amount: $5,000

No. of scholarships: 2

Website:
https://www.lafoundation.org/what-we-do/scholarships/student-scholarships/awards-available/landscape-forms-dei-scholarship

Requirements:

- Student who identifies as Black, Indigenous, and Person of Color
- Enrolled as undergraduate at a college or university
- Attending an accredited institution in the U.S. or Canada
- Majoring in landscape architecture or similar field of study

Society of Women Engineers Scholarship Program
Deadline: February 1 (college soph and above)
March 20 (entering college freshmen)

Award Amount: $1,000 to $10,000

No. of scholarships: Varies

Website:
https://scholarships.swe.org/applications/login.asp

Requirements:

- Women only
- Planning to study an ABET-accredited program in engineering, technology, or computing in the upcoming academic year
- Planning to attend full time (exceptions are made for reentry and non-traditional applicants)
- Not fully funded for tuition, fees, and books and equivalent

LasikPlus Scholarship
Deadline: February 2

Award Amount: $2,500

No. of scholarships: 1

Website: https://www.lasikplus.com/scholarship/

Requirements:

- U.S. citizen or legal permanent resident
- Enrolled full-time as an undergraduate or graduate student
- Currently enrolled at an accredited university in the U.S. or its territories
- Minimum 2.5 GPA

Jimmy Rane Foundation

Deadline: February 8

Award Amount: $500 to $5,000

No. of scholarships: Varies

Website:
https://www.jimmyranefoundation.org/scholarship

Requirements:

- U.S. citizen or permanent resident
- No older than 20 as of August 1
- Graduating high school senior or college student at accredited college/university
- 3.0 GPA for graduating high school senior/2.75 GPA for college student
- Resident of one of the following states: AL, AR, DC, DE, FL, GA, IA, KS, KY, LA, MD, MO, MS, NC, NE, NJ, NY, OH, OK, PA, SC, TN, TX, VA, WV
- Student athletes are *not* eligible

RMEL Foundation Scholarship

Deadline: February 9

Award Amount: $1,000 to $3,000

No. of scholarships: Varies

Website:
https://www.rmelfoundation.org/scholarships/

Requirements:

- U.S. citizen or permanent resident
- High school senior, high school graduate, or college undergraduate
- Be pursuing or plan to pursue an undergraduate degree with intent to pursue a career in the electric energy industry

George and Mary Josephine Hamman Foundation Scholarship

Deadline: February 16

Award Amount: $16,000 disbursed over four years

No. of scholarships: 70

Website:
http://hammanfoundation.org/scholarship-guidelines/

Requirements:

- Houston, Texas-area high school senior
- U.S. citizen
- Demonstrate academic ability and financial need

Optimist International Essay Contest

Deadline: February 28

Award Amount: Varies

No. of scholarships: Varies

Website:
http://www.optimist.org/e/member/scholarships3.cfm

Requirements: High school student under age of 18

Wells Fargo Veterans Scholarship Program

Deadline: February 28

Award Amount: Varies, renewable up to three years

No. of scholarships: Varies

Website:
https://learnmore.scholarsapply.org/wellsfargoveterans/

Requirements:

- Be honorably-discharged veteran or spouse of disabled veteran who served in the U.S. military, including the Reserves and National Guard, and have received a Certificate of Eligibility from the Department of Veterans Affairs or another document of service
- Be high school or GED graduate who plans to enroll or student already enrolled in full-time undergraduate or graduate study at an accredited two- or four-year college, university, or vocational-technical school
- Minimum 2.0 GPA
- Demonstrate financial need

LaGrant Foundation Undergraduate Scholarship

Deadline: February 29

Award Amount: $2,500

No. of scholarships: Varies

Website:
https://www.lagrantfoundation.org/scholarship-application-process

Requirements:

- Ethnic minority (African American, Asian American, Pacific Islander, Hispanic/Latino, Native American/Alaska Native)
- U.S. citizen or permanent resident
- Undergraduate college freshman, sophomore, junior or non-graduating senior
- Full-time student at four-year, accredited institution within the U.S., carrying a total of 12 units or more per semester/quarter
- Minimum 3.0 GPA
- Majoring in one of the following fields: Public relations, marketing or advertising, anthropology, communications, English, graphic design, or sociology
- If chosen, applicant MUST attend TLF's scholarship three-day summer activities to receive scholarship.

CHAPTER 10

SUBMIT MARCH – AUGUST SCHOLARSHIP APPLICATIONS

MARCH

Association For Women In Science (Seattle) Scholarship
Deadline: March 1

Award Amount: $1,000 to $5,000

No. of scholarships: 12

Website: http://seattleawis.org/award/scholarships/

Requirements:

- Applicants must have a U.S.-issued social security number
- College junior or senior at a four-year college or university
- State of Washington institution
- Declared major in the sciences, engineering or mathematics
- Demonstrated financial need

First Commonwealth Bank Scholarship
Deadline: March 1

Award Amount: $1,000

No. of scholarships: 35

Website:
https://www.fcbanking.com/why-us/community-commitment/scholarship/

Requirements:

- High school senior
- Resident of PA (Allegheny, Armstrong, Beaver, Bedford, Blair, Butler, Cambria, Clearfield, Elk, Indiana, Jefferson, Lawrence, Somerset, Washington or Westmoreland Counties) or OH (Ashtabula, Clermont, Delaware, Franklin, Hamilton, Madison or Stark Counties)
- Minimum 3.0 GPA

Gallery Collection Annual Create-A-Greeting-Card Scholarship Contest

Deadline: March 1

Award Amount: $10,000, plus $1,000 for school

No. of scholarships: 1

Website:
http://www.gallerycollection.com/greeting-cards-scholarship.htm

Requirements:

- U.S. citizen or legal resident
- Age 14 or older
- High school, college or university student

Hagan Scholarship

Deadline: March 1

Award Amount: $6,000 (Renewable)

No. of scholarships: Varies

Website: https://haganscholarships.org/

Requirements:

- U.S. citizen
- High school senior
- Attending an eligible public high school
- Minimum 3.75 GPA
- Enrolled or planning to enroll at an eligible four-year college or university the first semester following high school graduation
- Must work 240 hours prior to fall semester college enrollment
- Must apply for federal and state grants, if eligible
- Must not have a felony conviction

Rosa Parks Scholarship Foundation

Deadline: March 1

Award Amount: $2,000

No. of scholarships: 40

Website:
https://rosaparksscholarship.org/scholarship/apply/

Requirements:

- Michigan residents only
- High school senior graduating by August of the year of application
- Minimum 2.5 GPA

Society of Exploration Geophysicists (SEG) Foundation Scholarship

Deadline: March 1

Award Amount: Ranges from $500 to $14,000 per academic year

No. of scholarships: Varies

Website: http://seg.org/Scholarships

Requirements:

- High school senior; undergraduate or graduate college student
- Above average grades (merit-based)
- Planning to pursue a college curriculum directed toward a career in applied geophysics or a closely related field, such as geosciences, physics, geology, or earth and environmental sciences

Zeta Phi Beta National Educational Foundation

Deadline: March 2

Award Amount: $500 to $1,000

No. of scholarships: Varies

Website: https://z-nefscholarships.smapply.org/

Requirements:

- Graduating high school senior or undergraduate college student attending school full-time
- Minimum 3.0 GPA
- Demonstrate financial need

NOTE: Zeta chapters in most cities also offer local scholarships. Contact the chapter in your city for further details.

NSHSS First Generation Scholarship
Deadline: March 7

Award Amount: $1,000

No. of scholarships: 5

Website:
https://www.nshss.org/scholarships/s/nshss-first-generation-scholarship-2023-2024/

Requirement: First generation college students of all levels

Law Office of Philip W. Moore, Jr Leadership Excellence Scholarship
Deadline: March 12

Award Amount: $1,000

No. of scholarships: 1

Website: https://www.pwm-law.com/scholarship

Requirements:

- Enrolled in an undergraduate or graduate program at an accredited college or university within the U.S. for the upcoming semester
- At least 17 years of age
- Currently or will be in the future a member of student's university Greek life or honors program
- Minimum 3.0 GPA

Sigma Gamma Rho Sorority National Education Fund, Inc. Scholarship
Deadline: March 12

Award Amount: $500 to $2,000

No. of scholarships: Varies

Website:
https://www.sgrnationaleducationfund.org/scholarships

Requirements:

- High school senior or undergraduate student
- Demonstrate financial need

NOTE: SGRho chapters in most cities also offer local scholarships. Contact the chapter in your city for further details.

Claes Nobel Future Female Leader Scholarship
Deadline: March 14

Award Amount: $1,000

No. of scholarships: 10

Website:
https://www.nshss.org/scholarships/s/claes-nobel-future-female-leader-scholarship/

Requirements:

- High school senior
- Female student
- Minimum 3.5 GPA

Carroylin and Robert Threlkel Scholarship

Deadline: March 15

Award Amount: $1,000 to $5,000

No. of scholarships: Varies

Website:
https://sacregcf.academicworks.com/opportunities/637

Requirements:

- Female student
- Currently enrolled full-time in an accredited college, university or community college
- Pursuing a business-related undergraduate degree
- Minimum 2.5 GPA
- Demonstrate financial need

Eugene and Thora Chin Scholarship

Deadline: March 15

Award Amount: $1,000 to $5,000

No. of scholarships: Varies

Website:
https://sacregcf.academicworks.com/opportunities/641

Requirements:

- Asian/Pacific Islander heritage
- Plan to attend an accredited two- or four-year college, university, or graduate school
- Minimum 4.0 GPA in high school or 3.5 GPA in college
- Demonstrated financial need

Frame My Future Scholarship Contest
Deadline: March 15

Award Amount: $500 to $6,000

No. of scholarships: 4

Website:
https://www.diplomaframe.com/contests/frame-my-future-scholarship-contest-2022.aspx

Requirements:

- Legal U.S. citizen or resident
- Full-time student at a U.S. college or university

(The) Graydon and Myrth Fox Scholarship
Deadline: March 15

Award Amount: $1,000 to $5,000

No. of scholarships: Varies

Website:
https://sacregcf.academicworks.com/opportunities/631

Requirements:

- Veteran who has served honorably in the U.S. Armed Forces, a surviving spouse, dependent child or grandchild of a U.S. veteran
- Deceased or wounded personnel must have been performing official military duties in a combat situation or a military training exercise
- Pursuing a degree at an accredited college, university or trade school
- Demonstrate financial need

Hatfield Foundation Scholarship Program

Deadline: March 15

Award Amount: $5,000

No. of scholarships: 2

Website:
https://www.hatfieldfoundation.org/scholarship.html

Requirements:

- Be on track to complete high school in the current academic year
- Be on track to attend an accredited, 4-year university in the fall
- Have neither parent hold a bachelor's degree or higher
- Minimum 2.5 GPA
- Have attended at least one college readiness program during high school
- Have taken the SAT or ACT
- Have a demonstrated need for financial aid

Jonathan Dax Cooke Grant

Deadline: March 15

Award Amount: $1,000

No. of scholarships: 1

Website: https://daxcookegrant.com/apply/

Requirements:

- Strong academic achievement
- Minimum 2.5 GPA

National Restaurant Association Educational Foundation Scholarship

Deadline: March 15

Award Amount: $2,500

No. of scholarships: Varies

Website: https://chooserestaurants.org/scholarships

Requirements:

- U.S. citizen or permanent resident
- Full-time undergraduate college student
- Enrolled or accepted at an accredited post-secondary institution, college, or university
- Majoring in restaurant or hospitality industry-related field
- Plan to be enrolled for at least two consecutive terms

Pi Chi Omega Scholarship

Deadline: March 15

Award Amount: $2,000 to $3,000

No. of scholarships: 4

Website: http://www.pichiomega.org/scholarships/

Requirements:

- Full-time undergraduate or graduate college student
- Interested in a career in epidemiology, urban or industrial pest management
- Minimum 3.0 GPA

Quell Foundation Fighter Scholarship
Deadline: March 15

Award Amount: $7,500 to $10,000

No. of scholarships: 1

Website:
https://thequellfoundation.org/scholarships/

Requirements:

- High school senior or current undergraduate/graduate student
- Have been treated for a diagnosed mental health condition
- Minimum 3.2 GPA

Quell Foundation Survivor Scholarship
Deadline: March 15

Award Amount: $7,500 to $10,000

No. of scholarships: 1

Website:
https://thequellfoundation.org/scholarships/

Requirements:

- High school senior or current undergraduate/graduate student
- Have experienced the devastating loss of a parent, caregiver, or sibling to suicide
- Minimum 3.5 GPA

UNCF STEM Scholars Program

Deadline: March 19

Award Amount: $2,500 to $5,000

No. of scholarships: 100

Website: www.uncf.org

Requirements:

- African American
- High school senior
- U.S. citizen or permanent legal resident
- Majoring in engineering, mathematics, science or technology
- Minimum 3.0 GPA in math and science courses
- Demonstrated financial need

Trial Pro P.A. Scholarship

Deadline: March 20

Award Amount: $5,000

No. of scholarships: 1

Website: https://www.trialpro.com/scholarships/

Requirements:

- U.S. citizen or permanent resident
- Enrolled full time in high school, two-year college, four-year college/university, or master's degree program at an accredited university
- Minimum 3.0 GPA

TMCF/Acushnet Company Scholarship

Deadline: March 27

Award Amount: Up to $5,000

No. of scholarships: 10

Website: http://www.tmcf.org

Requirements:

- U.S. citizen or legal permanent resident
- Enrolled full-time as a freshman, sophomore, junior or senior
- Attending a Historically Black College or University (HBCU)
- Minimum 3.0 GPA
- Demonstrate financial need

TMCF/Bass Pro Shops & Cabela's Scholarship

Deadline: March 27

Award Amount: Up to $5,000

No. of scholarships: 4

Website: http://www.tmcf.org

Requirements:

- U.S. citizen or legal permanent resident
- Enrolled full-time as a junior or senior
- Attending a TMCF-member school (HBCU)
- Open to designated majors focusing on conservation or sustainability-related fields
- Minimum 3.0 GPA
- Demonstrate financial need

TMCF/Baxter STEM Scholarship

Deadline: March 27

Award Amount: Up to $20,000

No. of scholarships: 40

Website: http://www.tmcf.org

Requirements:

- U.S. citizen or legal permanent resident
- African American and/or of African descent
- Enrolled full-time a sophomore at an Historically Black College or University (HBCU)
- Open to STEM majors
- Minimum 3.0 GPA
- Demonstrate financial need

TMCF/Bridging the Dream Scholarship For Graduate School Students

Deadline: March 27

Award Amount: Up to $10,000

No. of scholarships: 10

Website: http://www.tmcf.org

Requirements:

- U.S. citizen or legal permanent resident
- Enrolled full-time or part-time at an accredited post-secondary institution in a graduate level program
- Be a diverse candidate, including but not limited to gender, disability, race, ethnicity, belonging to an underserved community
- Minimum 3.0 GPA

- Demonstrate leadership abilities
- Demonstrate good moral character in all aspects of your life, including personal, professional, educational, in your community, and online presence

TMCF/Bridging the Dream Scholarship For High School Seniors

Deadline: March 27

Award Amount: Up to $10,000

No. of scholarships: 25

Website: http://www.tmcf.org

Requirements:

- U.S. citizen or legal permanent resident
- Currently enrolled as a high school senior
- Plan to be a full-time college/university student in the upcoming academic year
- Plan to be enrolled at an accredited post-secondary institution or continuing education program, including two-year schools, four-year schools, or vocational/technical schools
- Be Pell Grant eligible
- Be a diverse candidate, including but not limited to gender, disability, race, ethnicity, belonging to an underserved community
- Minimum 2.75 GPA
- Demonstrate leadership abilities
- Demonstrate good moral character in all aspects of your life, including personal, professional, educational, in your community, and online presence

TMCF/CDW HBCU Scholarship

Deadline:	March 27
Award Amount:	Up to $5,000
No. of scholarships:	20
Website:	http://www.tmcf.org

Requirements:

- U.S. citizen or legal permanent resident
- Enrolled full-time as an undergraduate freshman, sophomore, junior or senior
- Attending a Historically Black College or University (HBCU)
- Minimum 3.0 GPA
- Demonstrate financial need

TMCF/Chime Scholarship

Deadline:	March 27
Award Amount:	Up to $5,000
No. of scholarships:	20
Website:	http://www.tmcf.org

Requirements:

- U.S. citizen or legal permanent resident
- Enrolled full-time as a freshman, sophomore, junior or senior
- Attending a TMCF-member school (HBCU)
- Minimum 3.0 GPA
- Demonstrate financial need

TMCF/CNA HBCU Scholarship
Deadline: March 27

Award Amount: Up to $8,000

No. of scholarships: 5

Website: http://www.tmcf.org

Requirements:

- U.S. citizen or legal permanent resident
- Enrolled full-time as an undergraduate junior or senior
- Attending a TMCF-member school (HBCU)
- Minimum 3.0 GPA
- Open to the following majors: Business, finance, statistics, mathematics, computer science and related majors
- Demonstrate financial need

TMCF/CoBank Agriculture Scholarship
Deadline: March 27

Award Amount: Up to $15,375

No. of scholarships: 8

Website: http://www.tmcf.org

Requirements:

- U.S. citizen or legal permanent resident
- Enrolled full-time as a freshman, sophomore, junior or senior
- Attending a TMCF-member school (HBCU)
- Open to students majoring in agriculture, banking, or finance

- Minimum 3.0 GPA
- Demonstrate financial need

TMCF/Coca Cola Foundation First Generation HBCU Scholarship

Deadline: March 27

Award Amount: Up to $6,000 (renewable)

No. of scholarships: 6

Website: http://www.tmcf.org

Requirements:

- U.S. citizen or legal permanent resident
- Be a graduating high school senior in the previous academic year
- Be a first generation college student in the upcoming academic year
- Enrolled full-time as an income freshman
- Attending a TMCF-member school (HBCU)
- Minimum 2.5 GPA
- Demonstrate financial need

TMCF/Cognizant Emerging Leaders Scholarship

Deadline: March 27

Award Amount: Up to $10,000

No. of scholarships: 13

Website: http://www.tmcf.org

Requirements:

- U.S. citizen or legal permanent resident
- Enrolled full-time as a freshman, sophomore, junior or senior
- Attending a TMCF-member school (HBCU)
- Preference given to students pursuing careers in technology and business
- Minimum 2.5 GPA
- Demonstrate financial need

TMCF/Conagra Scholarship

Deadline: March 27

Award Amount: Up to $5,000

No. of scholarships: 10

Website: http://www.tmcf.org

Requirements:

- U.S. citizen or legal permanent resident
- Enrolled full-time as an undergraduate junior or senior or MBA graduate student
- Attending a TMCF-member school (HBCU)
- Open to the following majors: Accounting, business, brand management, CIS, computer engineering, cybersecurity, finance, IT, math, marketing, supply chain, transportation, warehousing
- Minimum 3.0 GPA
- Demonstrate financial need

TMCF/Crème of Nature Legacy of Leadership Scholarship

Deadline: March 27

Award Amount: Up to $5,000

No. of scholarships: 20

Website: http://www.tmcf.org

Requirements:

- U.S. citizen or legal permanent resident
- Enrolled full-time as a freshman, sophomore, junior or senior
- Attending a Historically Black College or University (HBCU)
- Minimum 3.0 GPA
- Demonstrate financial need

TMCF/CVS Health Scholarship

Deadline: March 27

Award Amount: Up to $10,000

No. of scholarships: 5

Website: http://www.tmcf.org

Requirements:

- U.S. citizen or legal permanent resident
- Enrolled full-time as a freshman, sophomore, junior or senior
- Attending a TMCF-member school (HBCU)

- Open to undergraduate majors: Pre-Pharmacy, Biology, Pre-Medicine or Chemistry, Clinical Laboratory Science, Environmental Health, Health Administration, Health Information Management, Respiratory Therapy, Nursing, Behavioral Health, or Psychology
- Open to graduate majors: Master of Science in Pharmaceutical Science, Doctor of Philosophy (PhD) in Pharmaceutical Sciences, or Doctor of Pharmacy, Nursing, Behavioral Health, or Psychology
- Minimum 3.0 GPA
- Demonstrate financial need

TMCF/Deloitte Foundation HBCU Accounting Scholarship

Deadline:	March 27
Award Amount:	Up to $8,000/yr; $24,000 in total for 3 years
No. of scholarships:	70
Website:	http://www.tmcf.org

Requirements:

- U.S. citizen or legal permanent resident
- Enrolled full-time as an undergraduate freshman
- Attending a TMCF-member school (HBCU)
- Open to accounting majors
- Minimum 3.0 GPA
- Demonstrate financial need

TMCF/Directors Guild of America HBCU Scholarship

Deadline:	March 27
Award Amount:	Up to $10,250 (for up to 4 years, max up to $41,000)

No. of scholarships: 1

Website: http://www.tmcf.org

Requirements:

- U.S. citizen or legal permanent resident
- Enrolled full-time as a freshman, sophomore, junior, senior, or graduate student
- Attending a Historically Black College or University (HBCU)
- Open to students pursuing degrees (major or minor) in a film discipline
- Minimum 3.0 GPA
- Demonstrate financial need

TMCF/FedEx HBCU Scholarship

Deadline: March 27

Award Amount: Up to $8,000

No. of scholarships: 45

Website: http://www.tmcf.org

Requirements:

- U.S. citizen or legal permanent resident
- Enrolled full-time as a freshman, sophomore, junior or senior
- Attending a TMCF-member school (HBCU)
- Open to business majors
- Minimum 3.0 GPA
- Demonstrate financial need

TMCF/GCM Grosvenor Capital Management, L.P. HBCU Scholarship

Deadline: March 27

Award Amount: Up to $10,000

No. of scholarships: 7

Website: http://www.tmcf.org

Requirements:

- U.S. citizen or legal permanent resident
- Enrolled full-time as a freshman, sophomore, junior or senior
- Attending a TMCF-member school (HBCU)
- Minimum 3.0 GPA
- Demonstrate financial need

TMCF/ICON HBCU Scholarship

Deadline: March 27

Award Amount: Up to $10,625

No. of scholarships: 8

Website: http://www.tmcf.org

Requirements:

- U.S. citizen or legal permanent resident
- Enrolled full-time as a junior or senior
- Attending a TMCF-member school (HBCU)
- Open to the following majors: Data Analytics, Data Management, Life Sciences, Medicine, Nursing, Pharmacy, Statistics, STEM-related fields
- Minimum 3.0 GPA
- Demonstrate financial need

TMCF/J M Huber HBCU Scholarship
Deadline: March 27

Award Amount: Up to $10,000

No. of scholarships: 45

Website: http://www.tmcf.org

Requirements:

- U.S. citizen or legal permanent resident
- Enrolled full-time as a freshman, sophomore, junior or senior
- Attending a TMCF-member school (HBCU)
- Open to STEM majors
- Minimum 3.0 GPA
- Demonstrate financial need

TMCF/J P Morgan Chase Access Scholarship
Deadline: March 27

Award Amount: $10,000

No. of scholarships: 23

Website: http://www.tmcf.org

Requirements:

- U.S. citizen or legal permanent resident
- Enrolled full-time as a freshman, sophomore, junior or senior
- Attending a TMCF-member school (HBCU)
- Minimum 2.75 GPA
- Demonstrate financial need

TMCF/Jacobs HBCU Scholarship

Deadline: March 27

Award Amount: Up to $5,000

No. of scholarships: 10

Website: http://www.tmcf.org

Requirements:

- U.S. citizen or legal permanent resident
- Enrolled full-time as a freshman, sophomore, junior or senior
- Attending a TMCF-member school (HBCU)
- Open to the following majors: Architecture, Biology, Computer Information Systems, Computer Programming, Computer Science, Construction Management, Cybersecurity, Data Science, Ecology, Engineering (Aerospace, architectural, chemical, civil, computer, construction, electrical, environmental, general, geological, industrial, mechanical, nuclear, occupational safety, structural, or transportation), Environmental Health & Safety, Environmental Science, Fire Safety, Geology, Geographic Information Systems, Information Technology, Landscape Architecture, Occupational Safety, Health, or Environment, Safety Management, Supply Chain Management, Urban Planning
- Minimum 3.0 GPA
- Demonstrate financial need

TMCF/Lowe's Scholarship

Deadline: March 27

Award Amount: $500 up to $7,500

No. of scholarships: 60

Website: http://www.tmcf.org

Requirements:

- U.S. citizen or legal permanent resident
- Enrolled full-time as a sophomore, junior or senior
- Attending a TMCF-member school (HBCU)
- Have an unpaid school balance between $500 and $7,500
- Must not have previously received the Lowe's Scholarship
- Minimum 3.0 GPA
- Demonstrate financial need

TMCF/McDonald's Black and Positively Golden Scholarship

Deadline: March 27

Award Amount: Up to $15,000

No. of scholarships: 63

Website: http://www.tmcf.org

Requirements:

- U.S. citizen or legal permanent resident
- Enrolled full-time as an undergraduate freshman, sophomore, junior or senior
- Attending a Historically Black College or University (HBCU)
- Minimum 2.7 GPA
- Demonstrate financial need
- Demonstrate leadership abilities

TMCF/Medtronic Foundation Graduate/PhD Scholarship

Deadline: March 27

Award Amount: Up to $8,500

No. of scholarships: 5

Website: http://www.tmcf.org

Requirements:

- U.S. citizen or legal permanent resident
- Enrolled full-time as a graduate or PhD candidate
- Attending a Historically Black College or University (HBCU)
- Open to STEM majors only
- Minimum 3.0 GPA
- Demonstrate financial need

TMCF/Medtronic Foundation Undergraduate Scholarship

Deadline: March 27

Award Amount: Up to $8,500

No. of scholarships: 45

Website: http://www.tmcf.org

Requirements:

- U.S. citizen or legal permanent resident
- Enrolled full-time as a freshman, sophomore, junior or senior
- Attending a Historically Black College or University (HBCU)
- Open to STEM majors only

- Minimum 3.0 GPA
- Demonstrate financial need

TMCF/Mondelez International HBCU Scholarship
Deadline: March 27

Award Amount: Up to $9,000

No. of scholarships: 15

Website: http://www.tmcf.org

Requirements:

- U.S. citizen or legal permanent resident
- Be a graduating high school senior
- Enrolled full-time as an incoming freshman for the upcoming academic year
- Attending a TMCF/HBCU member-school
- Minimum 3.0 GPA
- Demonstrate financial need

TMCF/Palo Alto Networks Cyber Scholars Program
Deadline: March 27

Award Amount: Up to $10,000

No. of scholarships: 14

Website: http://www.tmcf.org

Requirements:

- U.S. citizen or legal permanent resident
- Enrolled full-time as an undergraduate or a graduate student at a public or private HBCU

- Attending a Historically Black College or University (HBCU)
  Preference will be given to those applicants enrolled in technology-related STEM or business disciplines
- Minimum 2.5 GPA
- Demonstrate financial need

TMCF/PPG Industries HBCU Scholarship
Deadline: March 27

Award Amount: Up to $10,000

No. of scholarships: 8

Website: http://www.tmcf.org

Requirements:

- U.S. citizen or legal permanent resident
- Enrolled full-time as an undergraduate junior or senior
- Attending a TMCF-member school (HBCU)
- Open to STEM related majors
- Minimum 3.0 GPA
- Demonstrate financial need

TMCF/Republic National Distributing Company Scholarship
Deadline: March 27

Award Amount: Up to $10,000

No. of scholarships: 5

Website: http://www.tmcf.org

Requirements:

- U.S. citizen or legal permanent resident
- Enrolled full-time as a college junior or senior
- Attending a select Historically Black College or University (HBCU)
- Open to the following majors: Business, hospitality management, marketing, sales
- Minimum 3.0 GPA
- Demonstrate financial need

TMCF/ServiceNow HBCU Scholarship

Deadline: March 27

Award Amount: Up to $8,200

No. of scholarships: 10

Website: http://www.tmcf.org

Requirements:

- U.S. citizen or legal permanent resident
- Enrolled full-time as a sophomore, junior or MBA graduate student
- Attending a TMCF-member school (HBCU)
- Open to the following majors: Business, communications, technology, engineering, math, humanities
- Minimum 2.75 GPA
- Demonstrate financial need

TMCF/Strategic Investment Group Alpha Scholarship

Deadline: March 27

Award Amount: Up to $3,000

No. of scholarships: 7

Website: http://www.tmcf.org

Requirements:

- U.S. citizen or legal permanent resident
- Enrolled full-time as an undergraduate junior or senior
- Attending a TMCF-member school (HBCU)
- Open to finance, economics, or accounting majors interested in a career in the capital market investments industry
- Minimum 3.0 GPA
- Demonstrate financial need
- Demonstrate leadership abilities

TMCF/Toyota Scholars Plus HBCU Scholarship

Deadline: March 27

Award Amount: Up to $10,000

No. of scholarships: 20

Website: http://www.tmcf.org

Requirements:

- U.S. citizen or legal permanent resident
- Enrolled full-time as a freshman, sophomore, junior or senior
- Attending a TMCF-HBCU member school
- Open to majors in finance, accounting, and other business majors; engineering, IT, computer science and other STEM majors
- Minimum 3.0 GPA
- Demonstrate financial need
- Demonstrate leadership abilities

TMCF/Truist Access Scholarship

Deadline: March 27

Award Amount: Up to $10,000

No. of scholarships: 45

Website: http://www.tmcf.org

Requirements:

- U.S. citizen or legal permanent resident
- Enrolled full-time as a freshman, sophomore, junior or senior
- Attending an Historically Black College or University (HBCU)
- Minimum 2.8 GPA
- Demonstrate financial need
- Demonstrate leadership abilities

TMCF/United Health Foundation Diversity in Health Care Scholarship

Deadline: March 27

Award Amount: Up to $5,000/yr for up to 4 years

No. of scholarships: 60

Website: http://www.tmcf.org

Requirements:

- U.S. citizen or legal permanent resident
- Identify as Black/African American, Hispanic/Latino, Native American/Alaska Native, or Asian, or is focused on the health of these communities or other underrepresented racial/ethnic groups

- Enrolled full-time as an undergraduate sophomore, junior, senior, or graduate and/or professional student
- Attending a Historically Black College or University (HBCU)
- Must have at least two years of study before their anticipated degree completion date
- Open to students pursuing degrees that will lead to careers as clinical professionals, including physician, physician assistant, nurse practitioner, certified nurse midwife, nurse, pharmacist, dentist, social worker, addiction counselor, clinical psychologist, or related clinical profession
- Minimum 3.0 GPA
- Demonstrate financial need

TMCF/Vanguard Scholarship

Deadline: March 27

Award Amount: Up to $5,000

No. of scholarships: 10

Website: http://www.tmcf.org

Requirements:

- U.S. citizen or legal permanent resident
- Enrolled full-time as an undergraduate junior
- Attending a TMCF-member school (HBCU)
- Open to the following majors: Accounting, business, communications, computer sciences, finance, graphic design, IT, math, statistics, STEM, supply chain
- Minimum 3.0 GPA
- Demonstrate financial need

TMCF/Verisk Scholarship

Deadline: March 27

Award Amount: Up to $10,625

No. of scholarships: 2

Website: http://www.tmcf.org

Requirements:

- U.S. citizen or legal permanent resident
- Enrolled full-time as a freshman, sophomore, junior or senior
- Attending a TMCF-HBCU member school
- Minimum 3.0 GPA
- Demonstrate financial need

TMCF/Westrock HBCU Scholarship

Deadline: March 27

Award Amount: Up to $10,000

No. of scholarships: 14

Website: http://www.tmcf.org

Requirements:

- U.S. citizen or legal permanent resident
- Enrolled full-time as an undergraduate sophomore, junior or senior
- Attending a Historically Black College or University (HBCU)
- Open to the following majors: Engineering (chemical, mechanical, electrical, or industrial), Pulp/paper science, Accounting/finance, Supply Chain
- Minimum 3.0 GPA

BMO Capital Markets Lime Connect Equity Through Education Scholarship

Deadline: March 28

Award Amount: $10,000

No. of scholarships: Varies

Website: https://www.limeconnect.com/programs/page/bmo-capital-markets-lime-connect-equity-through-education-scholarship

Requirements:

- Person with a (visible or non-visible) disability
- Current undergraduate or graduate student
- Attending a four-year university in the U.S. or Canada as a full-time student
- Pursuing a degree in business/commerce, computer science, engineering, math, physics, statistics, or a related discipline
- Interested in a career in Financial Services with a focus on Capital Markets preferred

Dechtman Wealth Management National Scholarship

Deadline: March 30

Award Amount: $3,500

No. of scholarships: 1

Website: https://dechtmanwealth.com/scholarship/

Requirements:

- Undergraduate student
- Attending a two- or four-year accredited American college

UBS-Paine Webber/UNCF Scholarship
Deadline: March 30

Award Amount: Up to $8,000

No. of scholarships: Varies

Website: http://www.uncf.org

Requirements:

- U.S. citizen, national, or permanent resident
- College sophomore or junior
- Enrolled at a UNCF-affiliated institution
- Minimum 3.0 GPA
- Majoring in accounting, business, business-related, economics, finance, international business, management or marketing

Active Life Scholarship for Financial Literacy
Deadline: March 31

Award Amount: $1,000

No. of scholarships: 1

Website:
http://www.getupgetactive.org/scholarship/

Requirements: Current college, graduate school or adult learners

Albert W. Dent Graduate Student Scholarship
Deadline: March 31

Award Amount: $5,000

No. of scholarships: 15

Website:
https://www.ache.org/career-resource-center/special-groups/resources-for-students-and-early-careerists

Requirements:

- U. S. citizen
- Minority student
- Enrolled full-time in a healthcare management graduate program—MHA, MPH, MBA in healthcare administration or similar
- Entering final year of full-time study
- Demonstrate financial need

Callender-Pritchard Legacy Scholarship
Deadline: March 31

Award Amount: $1,000

No. of scholarships: 1

Website: http://nanbpwc.org/education/

Requirements:

- African American graduating high school senior or recent high school graduate
- U.S. citizen
- Minimum 3.0 GPA
- Preferred majors: Political science, sociology, black studies

Congressional Black Caucus (CBC) Spouses Performing Arts Scholarship

Deadline: March 31

Award Amount: $5,000

No. of scholarships: Varies

Website:
https://cbcfinc.academicworks.com/opportunities/1068

Requirements:

- African-American student
- U.S. citizen or legal permanent resident
- Preparing to pursue or currently pursuing an undergraduate, graduate or doctoral degree full-time at an accredited college or university. Current high school seniors are also eligible to apply.
- Be pursuing a career in the performing arts with an eligible major
- Minimum 2.5 GPA
- Exhibit leadership and be active community

Congressional Black Caucus (CBC) Spouses Visual Arts Scholarship

Deadline: March 31

Award Amount: $5,000

No. of scholarships: Varies

Website:
https://cbcfinc.academicworks.com/opportunities/1070

Requirements:

- African-American student
- U.S. citizen or legal permanent resident
- Preparing to pursue or currently pursuing an undergraduate, graduate or doctoral degree full-time at an accredited college or university. Current high school seniors are also eligible to apply.
- Be pursuing a career in the visual arts with an eligible major
- Minimum 2.5 GPA
- Exhibit leadership and be active community

Don't Mess With Texas Scholarship

Deadline: March 31

Award Amount: Grand Prize - $6,000; Two additional $2,000 scholarships

No. of scholarships: 3

Website:
http://www.dontmesswithtexas.org/education-overview/scholarships/

Requirements:

- High school senior
- Current Texas resident
- Planning to pursue a two- or four-year degree at an accredited Texas college or university

Dr. Julianne Malveaux Scholarship

Deadline: March 31

Award Amount: $1,000

No. of scholarships: 1

Website: http://nanbpwc.org/education/

Requirements:

- African American female
- College sophomore or junior enrolled in an accredited college or university
- Majoring in journalism, economics, or related field
- U.S. citizen
- Minimum 3.0 GPA

Driver Education Initiative Scholarship

Deadline: March 31

Award Amount: $1,000

No. of scholarships: 1

Website: http://www.dmvedu.org/scholarship/

Requirements:

- High school sophomore, junior, senior, or college freshman
- Enrolled as a full-time student

Folds of Honor First Responder Scholarship

Deadline: March 31

Award Amount: Up to $5,000

No. of scholarships: Varies

Website:
https://foldsofhonor.org/scholarships/first-responder-scholarships/

Requirements: Spouses and children of fallen or disabled first responders

Irma A. Fleming Legacy Scholarship

Deadline: March 31

Award Amount: $1,000

No. of scholarships: 1

Website: http://nanbpwc.org/education/

Requirements:

- African American female
- Age 30-45 and finishing a degree
- U.S. citizen
- Minimum 3.0 GPA

Key Thinkers Scholarship

Deadline: March 31

Award Amount: $2,500

No. of scholarships: 1

Website: https://www.moneykey.com/scholarship/

Requirements:

- U.S. citizen or permanent resident
- 18 years or older
- Enrolled as a full-time student at an accredited college, university, or trade school in the U.S.
- Minimum 3.0 GPA

Lighthouse Guild Scholarship for the Legally Blind

Deadline: March 31

Award Amount: $10,000

No. of scholarships: 17

Website:
https://www.lighthouseguild.org/patients-families/scholarships/

Requirements:

- U.S. citizen or permanent resident
- Legally blind
- High school senior who will be incoming college freshman for upcoming academic year

National Association of Negro Business and Professional Women's Clubs, Inc. (NANBPWC) National Scholarship

Deadline: March 31

Award Amount: $1,000

No. of scholarships: 1

Website: http://nanbpwc.org/education/

Requirements:

- African American student
- U.S. citizen
- Graduating high school senior
- Minimum 3.0 GPA

OppU Achievers Scholarship

Deadline: March 31

Award Amount: $2,500

No. of scholarships: 1

Website: https://www.opploans.com/scholarship/

Requirements:

- U. S. citizen
- Enrolled full-time in high school or at least part-time in college, graduate, professional, or trade school
- Minimum 3.0 GPA

Sherelle T. and Timothy T. Carter III Scholarship

Deadline: March 31

Award Amount: $1,000

No. of scholarships: 1

Website: http://nanbpwc.org/education/

Requirements:

- African American single mother
- Age 18-30
- U.S. citizen
- Undergraduate student enrolled in an accredited college or university
- Majoring in a STEM, aviation, political science, communications, or business management related field

Stephen Feinberg Scholars Scholarship Program
Deadline: March 31

Award Amount: $20,000

No. of scholarships: Varies

Website:
https://cbcfinc.academicworks.com/opportunities/1074

Requirements:

- African-American student
- U.S. citizen or legal permanent resident
- Preparing to pursue or currently pursuing an undergraduate, graduate or doctoral degree full-time at an accredited college or university. Current high school seniors are also eligible to apply.
- Minimum 3.0 GPA
- Exhibit leadership and be active community

APRIL

Alzheimer's Foundation for America Teens for Alzheimer's Awareness College Scholarship
Deadline: April 1

Award Amount: $500 to $5,000

No. of scholarships: 10

Website:
https://alzfdn.org/young-leaders-of-afa/alzheimers-awareness-scholarship/

Requirements:

- U.S. citizen or permanent resident
- High school senior
- Must enter a four-year accredited college or university within 12 months of the application deadline

The Charles, Lela and Mary Slough Foundation Scholarship

Deadline: April 1

Award Amount: Up to $5,000 per year for a total of 5 years

No. of scholarships: Varies

Website:
https://mama.midland.edu/cc3_scripts/cc_server.exe

Requirements:

- Texas resident only
- Student entering or enrolled in accredited colleges/universities anywhere in the U.S.
- Demonstrate financial need

Davis-Putter Scholarship

Deadline: April 1

Award Amount: $1,000 to $10,000

No of scholarships: 30

Website:
http://www.davisputter.org/apply/apply-for-scholarships/

Requirements:

- High school senior, or college/university student at the undergraduate or graduate level
- Demonstrate financial need
- Must be active in a movement for social and/or economic justice

Delta Sigma Theta Research and Educational Foundation/Mentoring Keys Scholarship

Deadline: April 1

Award Amount: $5,000 over a two-year period

No. of scholarships: Varies

Website:
https://deltafoundation.net/scholarship-internship-opportunities/

Requirements:

- High school seniors and/or undergraduate students
- Attend Historically Black College or University (HBCU)
- Minimum 3.0 GPA
- Student pursuing a bachelor's degree in business related disciplines
- Multiple scholarships available, some with residency requirements in specific states

NOTE: Delta chapters in most cities also offer local scholarships. Contact the chapter in your city for further details.

Driven Coffee Scholarship
Deadline: April 1

Award Amount: $500

No. of scholarships: 1

Website:
https://www.drivencoffee.com/scholarship/

Requirement: Enrolled full-time at a college or university within the U.S. or Canada

Herbert Lehman Education Fund Scholarship
Deadline: April 1

Award Amount: $2,000/year for four years

No. of scholarships: Varies

Website:
http://www.naacpldf.org/herbert-lehman-education-fund-scholarship

Requirements:

- African American
- U.S. citizen
- High school senior, high school graduate, student entering college for first time or beginning their sophomore year in college
- Attending accredited four-year college/university

Project Yellow Light Scholarship (Sponsored by Mazda)
Deadline: April 1

Award Amount: $2,000 to $8,000

No. of scholarships: 6

Website: http://projectyellowlight.com/

Requirements: High school junior or senior, or undergraduate student at two- to four-year accredited college/university or technical school

Maineri Law Firm Higher Education Scholarship

Deadline: April 3

Award Amount: $1,000

No. of scholarships: 1

Website: https://www.mainerilaw.com/scholarship

Requirements:

- U.S. citizen or lawful permanent resident
- Currently enrolled in a college undergraduate program
- At least 17 years old
- Minimum 3.0 GPA
- Planning to pursue graduate degrees in one of the following fields: Communications, Education, Environmental Studies, Geography, Geology, History, Journalism, Language, Literature, Political Science, Psychology

Allegra Ford Thomas Scholarship

Deadline: April 5

Award Amount: $5,000 for two years ($2,500/year)

No. of scholarships: 1

Website:
https://www.ncld.org/scholarships-awards/

Requirements:

- Graduating high school senior
- Diagnosed with a documented learning disability (LD) and/or ADHD
- Enrolled in a two-year community college, a vocational or technical training program, or a specialized program for students with LD and/or ADHD

Anne Ford Scholarship
Deadline: April 5

Award Amount: $10,000 ($2,500/yr over four years)

No. of scholarships: 1

Website:
https://www.ncld.org/scholarships-awards/

Requirements:

- Graduating high school senior
- Diagnosed with a documented learning disability (LD) and/or ADHD
- Enrolled in a full-time bachelor's degree program

Raytheon Technologies SPY-6 Scholarship
Deadline: April 7

Award Amount: $10,000

No. of scholarships: 2

Website:
https://studentveterans.org/programs/scholarships?layout=edit&id=733

Requirements:

- Navy/Navy Reserve veteran
- Current student veteran
- Entering sophomore, junior, or senior year of undergraduate study, or be enrolled in a graduate program for the upcoming academic year
- Attending full-time at an accredited four-year college or university in the U.S.

Johnnie T. Melia Memorial Scholarship
Deadline: April 11

Award Amount: $1,000

No. of scholarships: 1

Website:
https://www.jtmeliamoving.com/jt-melia-scholarship-information-a-469.html

Requirement:

- High school or college student that intends to take college courses during the upcoming fall semester

Alfred Street Baptist Church HBCU/UNCF Scholarship
Deadline: April 15

Award Amount: $1,000 to $30,000

No. of scholarships: 88

Website: https://www.uncf.org

Requirements:

- U.S. citizen, national, or permanent resident
- Enrolled full-time as a degree-seeking student
- Attending any UNCF member institution or an HBCU
- Minimum 2.5 GPA
- Demonstrate unmet financial need

Alpha Kappa Alpha (AKA) Capitalized Endowment Fund Scholarships

Deadline: April 15

Award Amount: Varies

No. of scholarships: Varies

Website:
https://akaeaf.org/scholarships

Requirements:

- Full-time, college sophomore or beyond, including graduate students
- Enrolled at accredited degree-granting institution
- Minimum 3.0 GPA for merit-based scholarships; 2.5 GPA for financial need-based scholarships
- Demonstrate community service and involvement

NOTE: AKA chapters in most cities also offer local scholarships. Contact the chapter in your city for further details.

American Association of Blacks in Energy Scholarship
Deadline: April 15

Award Amount: $5,000

No. of scholarships: Varies

Website:
http://aabe.org/index.php?component=pages&id=4

Requirements:

- Minority student
- High school senior
- Entering an accredited college/university
- Minimum 3.0 GPA
- Majoring in business, technology, engineering, mathematics, or one of the physical sciences

Charles & Lucille King Family Foundation Scholarship
Deadline: April 15

Award Amount: Up to $7,000

No. of scholarships: Varies

Website:
https://www.unigo.com/scholarships/by-major/film-scholarships/king-family-foundation-scholarship/2932

Requirements:

- College sophomore or junior
- Full-time student
- Majoring in television and film
- Minimum 3.0 GPA

Children's Cause for Cancer Advocacy Scholarship

Deadline: April 15

Award Amount: $2,000

No. of scholarships: 2

Website: https://www.childrenscause.org/scholars/

Requirements:

- Childhood cancer survivor
- U.S. citizen or legal resident
- Age 25 or under
- Pursuing a bachelor's degree or higher

College Jumpstart Scholarship

Deadline: April 15

Award Amount: $1,000

No. of scholarships: 1

Website: http://www.jumpstart-scholarship.net/

Requirements:

- U.S. citizen or legal resident
- High school sophomore, junior, senior, college student, or non-traditional student
- Attend or plan to attend an accredited 2-year, 4-year, or vocational/trade school in the U.S.
- Be committed to using education to better your life and that of your family and/or community

DiBella Law Offices, P.C. Scholarship
Deadline: April 15

Award Amount: $500

No. of scholarships: 1

Website:
https://www.dibellalawoffice.com/scholarship/application.php

Requirements:

- High school senior or undergraduate student
- U.S. citizen or permanent resident
- Minimum 3.0 GPA

National Society of High School Scholars Foundation
Deadline: April 15

Award Amount: $1,000

No. of scholarships: 25+

Website:
https://nshssfoundation.org/scholarships/

Requirements:

- High school senior
- Minimum 3.0 GPA

William E. Wilson Graduate School Scholarship
Deadline: April 15

Award Amount: $5,000

No. of scholarships: 1

Website:
https://www.setc.org/scholarships

Requirements:

- Legal resident of one of the following states: AL, FL, GA, KT, MS, NC, SC, TN, VA, or WV
- At least one year of experience as a full-time teacher and director of theatre in a secondary school in one of the above states
- Enrolled in an accredited graduate program within one of the above states within one year of being selected for scholarship

Negative Population Growth Undergraduate Essay Scholarship

Deadline: April 18

Award Amount: $1,000 to $2,500

No. of scholarships: Varies

Website:
https://npg.org/2024-undergraduate-essay-scholarship-contest.html

Requirements:

- U.S. citizen or legal permanent resident
- Age 14 or older
- High school senior, or college freshman, sophomore or junior
- Enrolled in or attending an accredited school within the U.S. or operated overseas by the U.S. government

Negative Population Growth Graduate Students Essay Scholarship
Deadline: April 18

Award Amount: $1,000 to $5,000

No. of scholarships: Varies

Website:
https://npg.org/2024-undergraduate-essay-scholarship-contest.html

Requirements:

- U.S. citizen or legal permanent resident
- Age 14 or older
- Enrolled in an accredited graduate program of study, located within the U.S. or operated overseas by the U.S. government

Brave of Heart Scholarship
Deadline: April 20

Award Amount: $5,000 to $50,000

No. of scholarships: 100+

Website:
https://learnmore.scholarsapply.org/braveofheart/

Requirements:

- U.S. citizen or legal resident living in and attending an educational institution in the U.S. or a U.S. territory
- Be a child, spouse, or domestic partner of a frontline healthcare worker who lost their life to a COVID-19 related cause

- Plan to enroll full-time or part-time in an undergraduate or graduate program
- Plan to attend an accredited vocational-technical school, two- or four-year college or university, or graduate school
- Minimum 2.0 GPA

Atlas Shrugged Essay Contest

Deadline: April 25

Award Amount: First prize - $2,000; 5 Second Prizes - $500; 10 Third Prizes - $200; 45 Finalists - $50; 175 Semifinalists - $30

No. of scholarships: 236 Total

Website:
https://www.aynrand.org/students/essay-contests

Requirements:

- Open to students worldwide
- Eighth, ninth and tenth graders

Ally Financial Law Scholars Program

Deadline: April 27

Award Amount: $60,000

No. of scholarships: Varies

Website:
https://cbcfinc.academicworks.com/opportunities/1064

Requirements:

- African-American student
- U.S. citizen or legal permanent resident

- Full-time scholar at an accredited college or university
- Graduating senior entering law school upon receiving undergraduate degree
- Undergraduate alumni entering law school as a first-year law scholar
- Minimum 3.0 GPA
- Exhibit leadership and be active community

Congressional Black Caucus (CBC) Spouses Education Scholarship

Deadline: April 28

Award Amount: Varies

No. of scholarships: Varies

Website:
https://cbcfinc.academicworks.com/opportunities/1078

Requirements:

- African-American student
- U.S. citizen or legal permanent resident
- Permanent residence or attend academic institution in a CBC member's district
- Preparing to pursue or currently pursuing an undergraduate, graduate or doctoral degree full-time at an accredited college or university. Current high school seniors are also eligible to apply.
- Minimum 2.5 GPA
- Exhibit leadership and be active community

CVS Health Foundation Health Care Careers/UNCF Scholarship

Deadline: April 28

Award Amount: Up to $20,000

No. of scholarships: 45

Website: https://www.uncf.org

Requirements:

- U.S. citizen, national, or permanent resident
- African-American or Latino/Latina student
- College junior enrolled full-time at any U.S.-located accredited 4-year college or university
- Preference given to students attending an HBCU
- Pursuing a degree in a STEM-related discipline, such as biology, chemical engineering, chemistry, or mechanical engineering
- Have unmet financial need
- Minimum 3.0 GPA

Brown/MAE Health Care Scholarship

Deadline: April 30

Award Amount: $1,000

No. of scholarships: 1

Website: http://brownmae.org/scholarships/

Requirements:

- Minority student (African-American, Native American, Hispanic, or Asian-Pacific Islander)
- Interested in pursuing a health care career
- Minimum 3.0 GPA

Brown/MAE Teaching Scholarship

Deadline: April 30

Award Amount: $1,000

No. of scholarships: 1

Website: http://brownmae.org/scholarships/

Requirements:

- Minority student (African-American, Native American, Hispanic, or Asian-Pacific Islander)
- Interested in pursuing a teaching career
- Minimum 3.0 GPA

E-Waste Scholarship

Deadline: April 30

Award Amount: $500 to $1,500

No. of scholarships: 2

Website: http://www.digitalresponsibility.org/scholarships/

Requirements:

- U.S. citizen or legal resident
- High school student, undergraduate, or graduate college student

Joshua David Gardner Memorial Scholarship Endowment

Deadline: April 30

Award Amount: $2,000

No. of scholarships: 2

Website:
http://www.joshgardnerendowment.org

Requirements:

- African American
- Between ages of 17 and 25
- High school senior or college student
- Minimum 3.0 GPA
- SAT score of 1,500 or greater
- ACT score of 23 or greater

Norman O. Brown Scholarship
Deadline: April 30

Award Amount: $1,000

No. of scholarships: 1

Website: http://brownmae.org/scholarships/

Requirements:

- Minority student (African-American, Native American, Hispanic, or Asian-Pacific Islander)
- Minimum 2.0 GPA
- Demonstrate financial need

PCPS George Willie Ethnically Diverse Student Scholarship and Internship
Deadline: April 30

Award Amount: Up to $10,000

No. of scholarships: 10

Website:
https://thiswaytocpa.com/education/scholarship-search/georgewillie-scholarship-internship/

Requirements:

- U.S. citizen or permanent resident
- Ethnic minority student (African-American, Hispanic, Asian/Pacific Islander, or Native American)
- Senior student in college undergraduate accounting program
- Enrolled on a full-time basis and plan to remain enrolled full-time for the upcoming academic year
- Plan to pursue the CPA credential
- Completed at least 120 hours of course work and have 30 hours or fewer of upper-level accounting courses remaining
- Available for an internship during the accounting industry's busy season (January-April)

Shawn Carter Scholarship Foundation

Deadline: April 30

Award Amount: Up to $15,000

No. of scholarships: Varies

Website: http://www.shawncartersf.com

Requirements:

- U.S. citizen or permanent resident
- 25 years old or younger
- High school or college student, student with G.E.D. diploma or at vocational school
- Minimum 2.0 GPA
- Household income not exceeding $75,000

Soliant's Sunrise Scholarship

Deadline: April 30

Award Amount: $1,000

No. of scholarships: 1

Website:
http://www.soliantconsulting.com/about-soliant/soliants-sunrise-scholarship

Requirements:

- High school senior accepted to an accredited U.S. two-year or four-year college or university OR currently enrolled undergraduate student
- Minimum 3.0 GPA

MAY

Cancer Support Scholarship for Cancer Survivors

Deadline: May 1

Award Amount: Up to $5,000

No. of scholarships: 1

Website:
http://www.lepfoundation.org/#!applications/cihc

Requirements:

- U. S. citizen or resident
- Student diagnosed with cancer in childhood (letter of confirmation from physician required)
- Accepted or enrolled in a U.S. college or university

DutchCrafters Amish Furniture Heritage Scholarship
Deadline: May 1

Award Amount: $500

No. of scholarships: 3

Website:
http://www.dutchcrafters.com/heritage-scholarship

Requirements:

- U.S. citizen or legal resident
- High school or college student
- Enrolled in accredited four-year college/university
- Minimum 3.0 GPA
- Demonstrate financial need

Faith, Hope and Love Jesus Inc. Scholarship
Deadline: May 1

Award Amount: $500

No. of scholarships: 1

Website:
http://faithhopeandlovejesus.org/college_scholarship

Requirements:

- Student accepted or enrolled in an undergraduate program at an accredited college or university
- Physician's documentation of history of a blood disorder or cancer diagnosed before the age of 18

Helen Brett Scholarship

Deadline: May 1

Award Amount: Up to $5,000

No. of scholarships: Varies

Website:
https://www.iaee.com/helen-brett-scholarship/

Requirements:

- Full-time student enrolled at an accredited college, university, junior or technical college
- Enrolled in a degree program focusing on exhibition/event management
- Minimum 3.0 GPA

Ivey Engineering Scholarship

Deadline: May 1

Award Amount: $1,000

No. of scholarships: 1

Website:
https://www.iveyengineering.com/about-us/scholarship/

Requirements:

- High school senior
- Enrolled or planning to enroll as an undergraduate in a college or university inside the U.S. or Canada
- Students with full academic scholarships are not eligible to enter

John Lepping Memorial Scholarship for Disabled Youth
Deadline: May 1

Award Amount: Up to $5,000

No. of scholarships: 1

Website:
http://www.lepfoundation.org/#!applications/cihc

Requirements:

- Residents of NY, NJ or PA ONLY
- Disabled youth, including but not limited to physical disabilities and psychological handicaps (letter of confirmation from physician required)
- Accepted or enrolled in a U.S. college or university

Rover College Scholarship
Deadline: May 1

Award Amount: $2,500

No. of scholarships: 1

Website:
https://www.rover.com/college-scholarship/

Requirements:

- U.S. citizen or legal resident
- Graduating high school senior, undergraduate or community college student, or graduate student
- Minimum 3.0 GPA

Got A Spine Scholarship

Deadline: May 2

Award Amount: $500

No. of scholarships: 1

Website:
http://www.arcticchiropracticfairbanks.com/chiropractor_fairbanks.php

Requirements:

- U.S. or Canadian citizen
- High school senior or older
- Must plan to attend college full time by October
- Minimum 2.5 GPA

Thermo Scientific Pierce Scholarship Award

Deadline: May 1

Award Amount: $5,000 to $10,000

No. of scholarships: 6

Website:
http://www.pierce-antibodies.com/PierceScholarship/index.cfm

Requirements:

- Enrolled as an undergraduate or graduate student at an accredited college or university
- Minimum 3.0 GPA
- Majoring in biology, chemistry, biochemistry or a related life science field

Jack & Jill of America Foundation/UNCF Scholarship

Deadline: May 11

Award Amount: Up to $2,500

No. of scholarships: Varies

Website: http://www.uncf.org

Requirements:

- U.S. citizen or permanent resident
- African American student
- College freshman, sophomore, junior, or senior
- Accepted to or enrolled at accredited four-year college/university
- Minimum 3.0 GPA
- Majoring in communications
- Completed a minimum of 60 hours of active community service during junior and senior years of high school

Jimmy Beans for Brains Scholarship

Deadline: May 14

Award Amount: $2,500

No. of scholarships: 3

Website:
https://www.jimmybeanswool.com/details/knitting/scholarshipHome.asp

Requirements:

- High school senior, undergraduate, graduate, or professional school student
- Attending an accredited institution of higher education during the upcoming academic year
- Minimum 3.0 GPA
- Knowledge of knitting, crocheting, or weaving

Excellence in Accounting Undergraduate Scholarship Program

Deadline: May 15

Award Amount: $1,000

No. of scholarships: 1

Website:
https://www.alliancerecruitmentagency.com/excellence-accounting-scholarship-program-undergraduate/

Requirements:

- U.S. or Canadian citizen or permanent resident
- Undergraduate student at an accredited college or university
- Majoring in accounting
- Completed a minimum of 72 credit hours and at least one semester of the college's intermediate accounting course
- Minimum 3.0 GPA

Steven Scher Memorial Scholarship for Aspiring Restauranteurs

Deadline: May 15

Award Amount: $8,000

No. of scholarships: Varies

Website:
https://www.jamesbeard.org/scholarships

Requirements:

- U.S. citizen or resident
- High school senior or graduate
- Planning to enroll or already enrolled full- or part-time during upcoming academic year
- Course of study leading to a certificate or degree at a licensed or accredited culinary school

Trotter Project's Chef Homaro Cantu Scholarship
Deadline: May 15

Award Amount: $10,000

No. of scholarships: Varies

Website:
https://www.thetrotterproject.org/scholarships

Requirements:

- High school senior or college student
- Culinary arts or hospitality management student
- Attending any accredited college/university in the U.S.
- Minimum 2.5 GPA

Trotter Project Pursuit of Excellence Scholarship
Deadline: May 15

Award Amount: $10,000

No. of scholarships: Varies

Website:
https://www.thetrotterproject.org/scholarships

Requirements:

- High school senior or college student
- Culinary arts or hospitality management student
- Attending any accredited college/university in the U.S.
- Minimum 2.5 GPA
- Demonstrate financial need

Enterprise Holdings Road Forward/UNCF Scholarship

Deadline: May 19

Award Amount: $12,222

No. of scholarships: 12

Website: https://www.uncf.org

Requirements:

- U.S. citizen, national, or permanent resident
- African-American student
- High school senior
- First-generation college student
- Enrolled full-time at an accredited UNCF member institution
- Minimum 2.75 GPA
- Demonstrate financial need

B. Davis Scholarship

Deadline: May 21

Award Amount: $1,000

No. of scholarships: 1

Website:
http://www.studentawardsearch.com/scholarships.htm

Requirements: High school junior or senior; undergraduate college student

AbbVie Cystic Fibrosis (CF) Scholarship
Deadline: May 24

Award Amount: $2,500 to $23,000

No. of scholarships: 40

Website: http://www.abbviecfscholarship.com

Requirements:

- Individuals who have CF only
- High school senior, undergraduate student or graduate student at master's level
- Currently enrolled or admitted to an undergraduate or graduate program for the coming fall semester

Cariloop's Caregiver Scholarship
Deadline: May 30

Award Amount: $1,000 to $2,500

No. of scholarships: 3

Website:
https://bold.org/scholarships/cariloops-caregiver-scholarship/

Requirement: Current college student who is the main caregiver in their family and/or community

Attorney Patrick Woolley Healthy Communities Scholarship

Deadline: May 31

Award Amount: $1,000

No. of scholarships: 1

Website:
https://virginialawfirm.net/2024-healthy-communities-scholarship/

Requirements:

- Currently enrolled in a course of study at any accredited community or junior college or an undergraduate or graduate degree program anywhere in the United States
- Minimum 3.0 GPA
- Demonstrate strong commitment to helping others and describe personal examples of a time they have encouraged sustainable and local health initiatives in local community

Jayda Dionne Parker Scholarship

Deadline: May 31

Award Amount: $1,000

No. of scholarships: 1

Website: http://www.jdpscholar.org/

Requirements:

- Current college student
- Attending an accredited college or university

JUNE

180 Medical Scholarship Program
Deadline: June 1

Award Amount: $1,000

No. of scholarships: 7

Website:
http://www.180medical.com/scholarships

Requirements:

- Must be under a physician's care for a spinal cord injury, spina bifida, transverse myelitis, neurogenic bladder, or ostomy (ileostomy, colostomy, or urostomy)
- U.S. citizen or legal resident
- Attending a two-year, four-year, or graduate school program full time in the upcoming fall semester

Bertolino Government Regulatory Impact Scholarship
Deadline: June 1

Award Amount: $2,500

No. of scholarships: 1

Website:
https://www.belolaw.com/about/government-regulations-scholarship/

Requirements:

- Resident of the United States
- At least 18 years old
- Enrolled at an accredited college, university, or graduate school
- Minimum 3.0 GPA
- In good academic standing

CVS Health Minority Scholarship for Pharmacy Students

Deadline: June 1

Award Amount: $8,000

No. of scholarships: 5

Website:
https://www.aacp.org/resource/cvs-health-minority-scholarship-pharmacy-students

Requirements:

- Underrepresented minority student (African-American, Hispanic or Latino, Native American, or Pacific Islander)
- U.S. citizen or DACA-approved
- Accepted into a PharmD program for the upcoming academic year
- Minimum 3.0 GPA
- Demonstrate leadership, academic success, and a commitment to advancing the pharmacy profession and patient care

Jane Austen Society of North America Essay Contest

Deadline: June 1

Award Amount: $250 to $1,000

No. of scholarships: 3

Website: http://jasna.org/essaycontest/index.html

Requirements: Open to full-time students worldwide at the high school, undergraduate or graduate levels

Law Offices of Scott Henry Scholarship
Deadline: June 1

Award Amount: $1,000

No. of scholarships: 1

Website:
https://topcriminallawfirm.com/2021-the-law-offices-of-scott-henry-scholarship/

Requirements:

- High school senior, undergraduate, graduate or law school student
- Minimum 3.0 GPA

Crowdstrike Foundation's NextGen Scholarship
Deadline: June 2

Award Amount: $7,500

No. of scholarships: 5

Website:
https://www.crowdstrike.com/about-crowdstrike/nextgen-scholarship-program/

Requirements:

- Currently enrolled as an undergraduate or graduate student
- Studying cybersecurity and/or artificial intelligence

PixelPlex STEM Scholarship
Deadline: June 5

Award Amount: $2,000

No. of scholarships: 1

Website: https://pixelplex.io/scholarship/

Requirements:

- U.S. citizen or permanent resident
- Enrolled or accepted in a college or university in the U.S.
- Field of study is related to science, technology, engineering, math, economics, or business

Duck Brand Duct Tape Stuck at Prom Scholarship
Deadline: June 7

Award Amount: $10,000 Grand Prize (2 winners)
$500 for 8 Runners Up

No. of scholarships: 10

Website:
https://www.duckbrand.com/stuck-at-prom

Requirements:

- Legal resident of the U.S., District of Columbia, Puerto Rico, and all U.S. territories and Canada (*excluding* MD, TN, CO, VT, NE, and ND)
- 14 years of age or older
- Enrolled in a high school or home school association at the high-school level

Akash Kuruvilla Memorial Scholarship Fund
Deadline: June 9

Award Amount: $1,000

No. of scholarships: 3

Website: https://akmscholarship.com

Requirements:

- High school senior or undergraduate student at accredited college/university
- Minimum 3.5 GPA for high school student; minimum 3.0 GPA for college student
- Demonstrate financial need

Abbott & Fenner Business Consultants Scholarship
Deadline: June 10

Award Amount: $1,000

No. of scholarships: 1

Website:
http://www.abbottandfenner.com/scholarships.htm

Requirements: High school junior or senior; college/university student at accredited institutions

Connect Her Film Festival Scholarship

Deadline: June 15

Award Amount: $1,000 to $5,000

No. of scholarships: Varies

Website: https://connectherfilmfest.org/submit/

Requirements:

- Females only
- Full-time high school student or enrolled undergraduate student
- Maximum age of 25 as of Dec. 31
- International students from all countries, including the U.S., with the exception of the following: Cuba, Iran, North Korea, Sudan and Syria

Koch Scholars/UNCF Program

Deadline: June 17

Award Amount: Up to $5,000

No. of scholarships: 200

Website: http://www.uncf.org

Requirements:

- African American
- U.S. citizen, permanent resident or foreign national

- High school senior
- Applying to or admitted to an eligible full-time four-year college or university. See website for list of eligible colleges/universities.
- Minimum 3.0 GPA
- Majoring in accounting, business, economics, engineering, history, philosophy or political science

Probo Medical Scholarship

Deadline: June 21

Award Amount: $500

No. of scholarships: 1

Website:
https://www.probomedical.com/probo-medical-scholarship/

Requirements:

- U.S. citizen
- Age 16 or older
- Current high school senior or undergraduate student
- Attending or planning to attend an accredited U.S. college or university
- Minimum 3.0 GPA

(The) Cove Scholarship Program

Deadline: June 30

Award Amount: $3,000

No. of scholarships: 1

Website:
https://www.covesmart.com/landing/scholarship/

Requirements:

- U.S. citizen
- Currently enrolled in an accredited 2- or 4-year college or university in the U.S.

Digital Privacy Scholarship
Deadline: June 30

Award Amount: $500 to $1,500

No. of scholarships: 2

Website:
http://www.digitalresponsibility.org/scholarships/

Requirements:

- U.S. citizen or legal resident
- High school student, undergraduate or graduate college student

Washington Media Scholars Foundation Mia Guion Scholarship
Deadline: June 30

Award Amount: $2,500

No. of scholarships: 1

Website:
https://www.mediascholars.org/mia-guion-scholarship/

Requirements:

- Currently enrolled at a U.S. college or university as an undergraduate student
- Majoring in advertising, marketing, communications, business, political science, strategic media
- Demonstrate financial need

JULY

AMVAC Cotton Industry Advancement Scholarship

Deadline: July 1

Award Amount: $2,000

No. of scholarships: 7

Website: https://www.amvac.com/scholarship

Requirements:

- High school senior or currently enrolled in an agricultural area of study at an accredited college or university
- Must be nominated by a cotton consultant and have worked for a cotton consultant at some point in the last two years

KB Delta Compressor Valve Parts Scholarship

Deadline: July 1

Award Amount: $1,000

No. of scholarships: 1

Website: http://kbdelta.com/scholarship.html

Requirements: Student enrolled in any accredited college or university

Kuru Footwear Scholarship
Deadline: July 1

Award Amount: $1,000

No. of scholarships: 1

Website:
https://www.kurufootwear.com/scholarship

Requirements:

- U.S. citizen
- Incoming freshman, college sophomore, junior, or senior
- Enrolled full-time at an accredited college or university
- Minimum 2.5 GPA

Larson Law Office Scholarship
Deadline: July 1

Award Amount: $1,000

No. of scholarships: 1

Website:
https://www.thelarsonlawoffice.com/scholarship/

Requirement: Currently enrolled or plan to attend a college, trade school, university, or graduate institution in the United States

Simeone Miller LLP Scholarship
Deadline: July 1

Award Amount: $1,000

No. of scholarships: 1

Website:
https://www.simeonemiller.com/scholarship/

Requirement: Currently enrolled or accepted as an undergraduate or law student

Creative Safety Supply Scholarship
Deadline: July 15

Award Amount: $1,000

No. of scholarships: 1

Website:
https://www.creativesafetysupply.com/scholarship/

Requirements:

- U.S. citizen or permanent resident
- Enrolled in a college, university, or vocational school for the upcoming term
- Minimum 3.0 GPA

Crystal Group Innovation Scholarship
Deadline: July 15

Award Amount: $1,000

No. of scholarships: 2

Website:
https://www.crystalrugged.com/scholarships/

Requirements:

- Enrolled full-time at an accredited two- or four-year institution in the U.S.
- Pursuing a bachelor's degree in an undergraduate business, engineering or related program
- Minimum 3.0 GPA
- Must have completed at least 60 semester hours

Sprout Social/UNCF Scholarship
Deadline: July 17

Award Amount: $11,000

No. of scholarships: 8

Website: https://www.uncf.org

Requirements:

- U.S. citizen, national, or permanent resident
- Attending an accredited four-year institution
- Enrolled as a full-time college senior for the upcoming academic year
- Minimum 3.0 GPA
- Preference granted to applicants attending Howard University, North Carolina A&T State University and Georgia Institute of Technology
- Majoring in computer science, software engineering, or a related field

R&D Systems Scholarship
Deadline: July 19

Award Amount: $1,500

No. of scholarships: 1

Website:
https://www.rndsystems.com/grants-scholarships/scholarship-application

Requirements:

- Student studying in a college/university within the U.S., Canada, and European countries only
- Enrolled or accepted for enrollment at the time of application
- Declared major in a science-related field (e.g., life science, medical science, health science, nursing, biology, chemistry, environmental sciences, medical engineering)

Cat Zingano Overcoming Loss Scholarship
Deadline: July 20

Award Amount: $10,000

No. of scholarships: 1

Website:
https://bold.org/scholarships/cat-zingano-scholarship/

Requirements:

- High school senior or college student at any level
- Student is fighting through the loss of a close family member, legal guardian or loved one, and is in need of financial support for future education

Anders Scholarship
Deadline: July 30

Award Amount: $1,000

No. of scholarships: 1

Website:
https://www.andersgroup.org/healthcare-scholarship

Requirements:

- Enrolled in a college or trade program
- Minimum 3.0 GPA

Bachus & Schanker, LLC Scholarship
Deadline: July 30

Award Amount: $2,000

No. of scholarships: 1

Website: http://www.coloradolaw.net/scholarship/

Requirements:

- High school senior or undergraduate student
- Accepted to or attending a four-year university
- Minimum 3.0 GPA

BK Law Group's Strong Work Ethic Scholarship
Deadline: July 31

Award Amount: $1,000

No. of scholarships: 1

Website:
https://bk-lawgroup.com/2021-strong-work-ethic-scholarship/

Requirements:

- U.S. citizen
- Current high school, undergraduate or graduate school student
- Enrolled in a two- to five-year post-secondary institution for the upcoming fall semester
- Minimum 3.0 GPA
- In good overall academic standing

CardRates.com Financial Futures Scholarship
Deadline: July 31

Award Amount: $1,000

No. of scholarships: 1

Website: https://www.cardrates.com/scholarship/

Requirements:

- U.S. resident
- High school senior or current college student
- Minimum 3.5 GPA
- Majoring in business, accounting, finance, mathematics, management, and others related to the personal finance industry

Earnest Scholarship
Deadline: July 31

Award Amount: $5,000

No. of scholarships: 5

Website:
https://www.earnest.com/student-loans/scholarship

Requirements:

- Enrolled or planning to enroll as a full-time student at an accredited U.S. college or university for the upcoming academic semester
- Domestic, international, undocumented and online students *are* eligible to apply
- No minimum GPA required

Gen and Kelly Tanabe Scholarship

Deadline: July 31

Award Amount: $1,000

No. of scholarships: 3

Website: http://www.genkellyscholarship.com

Requirements:

- U.S. citizen or legal resident
- High school student from 9th to 12th grade OR undergraduate or graduate college student

Semper Solaris Scholarship

Deadline: July 31

Award Amount: $500 to $3,000

No. of scholarships: 4

Website:
https://www.sempersolaris.com/semper-cares-initiative/scholarships/

Requirements:

- Current high school senior
- Enrolled full-time at an accredited high school
- Minimum 3.0 GPA

AUGUST

Driver Education Initiative Scholarship

Deadline: August 1

Award Amount: $1,000

No. of scholarships: 1

Website: http://www.dmvedu.org/scholarship/

Requirements:

- High school sophomore, junior, senior, or college freshman
- Enrolled as a full-time student

Jane M. Klausman Women in Business Scholarship

Deadline: August 1

Award Amount: $2,000 to $8,000

No. of scholarships: 32

Website:
https://www.zonta.org/Web/Programs/Education/Women_in_Business_Scholarship

Requirements:

- Female college student of any age enrolled in at least the second year of an undergraduate program through the final year of a Master's program
- Enrolled at an accredited university, college, or institute
- Pursuing a business program with major field of specialization in accounting, economics, finance, business management, marketing, operations management, human resources management, international business, or entrepreneurship

Patsy Takemoto Mink Education Foundation Scholarship

Deadline: August 1

Award Amount: Up to $5,000

No. of scholarships: 5

Website: http://www.patsyminkfoundation.org

Requirements:

- U. S. citizen
- Female
- Age 17 or order
- Mother, with minor children
- Enrolled in a skills training, ESL or GED program; or pursuing a technical/vocational degree, an associate's degree, a first bachelor's degree, or a graduate degree
- Low-income family household with annual income less than $17,500 for a family of 2; $22,000 for a family of 3; $26,500 for a family of 4

Stewart J. Guss College Student Scholarship
Deadline: August 1

Award Amount: $1,000

No. of scholarships: 1

Website:
http://attorneyguss.com/annual-stewart-j-guss-college-student-scholarship/

Requirements: Aspiring or current college student

James W. Lewis High School Global Leader Scholarship (NSHSS)
Deadline: August 5

Award Amount: $5,000

No. of scholarships: 5

Website:
https://www.nshss.org/scholarships/s/nshss-james-w-lewis-high-school-global-leader-scholarship/

Requirements:

- High school sophomore, junior, or senior
- Minimum 3.5 GPA
- Exemplify a commitment to diversity and inclusion, encouraging leadership among youth, and innovation and entrepreneurship

Job-Applications.com Working Parent College Scholarship
Deadline: August 11

Award Amount: $1,000

No. of scholarships: 1

Website:
https://www.job-applications.com/scholarships/

Requirements:

- Legal resident of the U.S.
- At least 18 years old
- Currently enrolled as a full or part-time student at an accredited U.S. post-secondary educational institution
- Minimum 3.0 GPA
- Worked an average of at least twelve (12) hours for each of the previous four (4) weeks at the time of applying
- Residential parent of at least one minor child

MarvelOptics National Scholarship Contest
Deadline: August 15

Award Amount: $1,500

No. of scholarships: 1

Website:
https://marveloptics.com/blog/scholarship-program/

Requirements:

- Current, full-time undergraduate student
- Attending an accredited two-year or four-year American college or university

Abacus Life Scholarship
Deadline: August 26

Award Amount: $1,000

No. of scholarships: 1

Website:
https://abacuslifesettlements.com/abacus-scholarship/

Requirements:

- Full-time or part-time college student
- Attending an accredited four-year college or university in the U.S.

Americanism Educational Leaders Essay Contest
Deadline: August 31

Award Amount: $1,000 to $2,500

No. of scholarships: 3

Website:
http://infoguides.pepperdine.edu/AEL

Requirements:

- U.S. citizen
- Undergraduate student at an accredited four-year U.S. college or university

Clubs of America Scholarship
Deadline: August 31

Award Amount: $1,500

No. of scholarships: 1

Website:
http://www.greatclubs.com/scholarship-award-for-career-success.asp

Requirements:

- Undergraduate student at accredited college/university
- Minimum 3.0 GPA

iVein Health & Wellness Scholarship
Deadline: August 31

Award Amount: $2,500

No. of scholarships: 1

Website: https://www.ivein.com/scholarship/

Requirements:

- Current full-time undergraduate/graduate student
- Attending an accredited U.S. university or college
- Minimum 3.7 GPA

National African-American Insurance Association JL Tillman Scholarship
Deadline: August 31

Award Amount: $3,000

No. of scholarships: 5

Website: https://www.naaia.org/scholarship

Requirements:

- U.S. citizen
- African-American student

- College-bound high school senior, current college/university student, or current community college student
- Minimum 2.5 GPA
- Pursuing a degree in insurance, risk management, business, actuarial science, finance, IT, or marketing and communications

Thurgood Marshall College Fund All Around Scholarship

Deadline: August 31

Award Amount: $10,000

No. of scholarships: 2

Website: https://www.tmcf.org

Requirements:

- U.S. citizen or legal permanent resident
- Enrolled full-time as a freshman, sophomore, junior, or senior
- Attending a TMCF-member school
- Minimum 3.0 GPA
- Demonstrate financial need

Tide.com Scholarship (Procter & Gamble)

Deadline: August 31

Award Amount: $10,000

No. of scholarships: 150

Website: https://tide.com/scholarship

Requirements: College-bound or existing college student

CHAPTER 11

PURSUE PAID INTERNSHIPS

As mentioned in Chapter 8, internships provide another avenue to earn much-needed funds for college. While some internships offer only course credit and do not provide monetary compensation, many of them include paid stipends, housing, and even salaries.

An internship for course credit offers needed exposure within the student's field of study, but a paid internship offers both the exposure and monetary rewards. A paid internship can provide much-needed funds for college expenses throughout the semester or academic year. Since the funds go directly to the student, they can be used for books, housing, transportation, clothing, laptops, and other expenses directly related to the student's college matriculation.

Internships can be available during the summer or during the academic year, usually for either the fall or spring semester. They are usually offered to college students during their junior and/or senior years once their course curriculum is more directly related to their chosen major or field of study. Some are also offered to graduate students in master's or doctoral programs and to students in law school or medical school. Being able to list an internship with a major corporation can go a long way toward favorable results in the scholarship award process and also for full-time employment after graduation.

The college or university the student attends is a good source for available internship opportunities. Check with the institution's career office or the academic advisor.

Following are some paid internships students may pursue:

Abbott Laboratories Internship
Website:
https://www.abbott.com/careers/students/internships.html

Requirements:

- Current undergraduate or graduate student having completed one year of college education before beginning internship
- Enrolled in school the semester/quarter following internship
- Excellent academic achievement
- Demonstrate exceptional interpersonal skills

Amazon Internship
Website:
https://www.amazon.jobs/en/business_categories/student-programs

Requirements:

- Current undergraduate or graduate student
- Majoring in technology, business, law, or human resources

American Express Undergraduate Summer Internship Program
Website:
https://www.americanexpress.com/en-us/careers/student-programs/us/?intlink=us-amex-career-en-us-home-usstudent

Locations: Various

Requirements:

- Undergraduate student studying Finance, Marketing, Technology, Strategy, and related fields.
- Entering senior year of college

Boeing Internships
Website:
https://jobs.boeing.com/internships#/internships

Requirements:

- Internships are available for students majoring in business, engineering, information technology, and data analytics
- Students may be enrolled in a bachelor's degree program, consolidated bachelor's/master's degree program, or master's degree program
- Students must commit to working full-time in 12-week programs

Caterpillar Corporate/Part-Time Internship
Website:
https://www.caterpillar.com/en/careers/career-areas/college/unitedstates/intern-program.html

Requirements:

- Full-time student at a four-year university
- Completed at least 12 semester hours
- Minimum 2.8 GPA
- Opportunities available in accounting, revenue management, communications, engineering, environmental health and safety, finance, human resources, information technology, supply chain, logistics, manufacturing/operations, marketing, analytics, and purchasing

Deloitte Internship
Website:
https://www2.deloitte.com/us/en/pages/careers/articles/join-deloitte-undergraduate-degree-opportunities.html

Requirements:

- High academic achievement
- Majoring in accounting or finance
- College undergraduate or graduate student

Dropbox Summer Internship
Website: https://jobs.dropbox.com/

Location: Remote (12 weeks)

Requirements:

- Undergraduate or graduate student
- Must be curious, reliable, and possess excellent communication skills
- Internships offered in design, engineering, project management, customer service, research/analyst, machine learning, and related fields.

Eastman Kodak Internship
Website:
https://www.kodak.com/en/company/page/careers-apprenticeships-internships

Requirements:

- High school student or full-time college student at the undergraduate or graduate level
- Interest in business, supply chain, chemical engineering, communications, journalism, computer science, analytics, or similar field
- Eager to work in a fast-paced environment

El Paso Electric Internship
Website:
https://www.epelectric.com/careers/summer-college-internship-program

Requirements:

- Currently enrolled full-time as an undergraduate or graduate student
- Enrolled at an accredited college or university in the U.S. and completed at least two (2) semesters
- Minimum 3.0 GPA and in good academic standing
- Pursuing an undergraduate or graduate degree in science, math, engineering, accounting, finance, business or related field
- Legally authorized to work in the U.S.

Federal Deposit Insurance Corporation (FDIC) Summer Legal Intern Program
Website:
https://www.fdic.gov/about/careers/student-opportunities/legal-intern-program.html

Locations: Washington, DC and Arlington, VA

Requirements:

- Currently enrolled in an accredited Juris Doctorate (JD) or LL.M program
- Completion of one full academic year of graduate level education OR eligibility under the Superior Academic Achievement Provision and completion of a bachelor's degree
- Minimum 2.5 GPA and remain in good academic standing

Hershey Entertainment & Resorts Internship
Website: https://www.hersheyjobs.com

Requirements:

- Possess strong communication skills
- Exhibit enthusiasm, professionalism, and a personal drive for success
- Interest in hospitality or tourism profession

Kansas City Monarchs Baseball Internship
Website: https://monarchsbaseball.com/internships/

Location: Kansas City, MO

Requirements:

- Undergraduate or graduate student
- Possess excellent communications skills, be self-motivated, and have strong customer service skills
- Internships offered in game day experience, social media, photography/videography, AV and production, media relations/broadcasting, corporate partnerships, hospitality, merchandise/retail, stadium operations, grounds/facilities, and tickets/sales.

Marsh & McLennan Companies Internship

Website: https://careers.mmc.com

Location: Washington, DC

Requirements:

- Rising college junior or senior
- Working toward a B.A. or a B.S. in any major
- High academic achievement
- Demonstrate exceptional analytical and critical thinking skills
- Coursework and/or experience in finance, economics, accounting, statistical analysis/econometrics, and computer programming preferred

Miami Heat Summer Internship Program

Website:
https://www.nba.com/heat/summerinternship

Location: Miami, FL

Requirements:

- College undergraduate or graduate student
- Internships offered in media production, control room, product marketing, marketing strategy, broadcast, data analytics, digital content, digital innovation strategy, email marketing and automation, and project management

Miller Cooper Internship Program
Website:
https://millercooper.com/internship-program/

Location:	Chicago, IL
Requirements:	College freshman or sophomore pursuing public accounting profession

National Air and Space Museum Summer Internship Program
Website:
https://airandspace.si.edu/support/get-involved/internships

Location:	Washington, DC
Requirements:	College student majoring in any field of study

NBC Universal Market Research/Programming Internship
Website:
https://jobs.universalparks.com/universal-orlando-resort/

Location:	Orlando, FL

Requirements:

- College sophomore, junior, or senior
- Pursuing an associate, bachelor, or graduate degree at an accredited institution
- Minimum 3.0 GPA
- Majoring in marketing, business, psychology, sociology, anthropology, or other social science

Nestle Sales Finance Internship

Website: https://www.nestlejobs.com/early-careers

Location: Bridgewater, NJ

Requirements:

- Students majoring in economics, accounting, finance, business, or related fields.
- Possess excellent Microsoft Office, analytical, interpersonal, communication, organizational, and time management skills

Omni Care Hospitality Internships

Website:
https://www.omnihotels.com/careers/omni-care-internships

Requirements:

- Undergraduate college student
- Interested in hospitality/food and beverage industry
- Must possess strong communication and customer service skills and be willing to adapt to changing environments

Price Waterhouse Coopers Internship
Website:
https://www.pwc.com/us/en/careers/entry-level/programs-events/start.html

Requirements:

- Ethnic minority
- College sophomore in a 4-year program, or a college sophomore or junior in a 5-year program
- Minimum 3.3 GPA
- Pursuing a bachelor's degree in accounting or a STEM major

Shell Oil Internship
Website:
https://www.shell.com/careers/about-careers-at-shell/assessed-internships.html

Requirements:

- Must be in penultimate year of study at a recognized university
- Studying toward a bachelor's or master's degree
- Possess a strong academic record

Target Corporation Internship
Website:
https://corporate.target.com/careers/internships.

Requirements:

- Recent college graduate or seeking internship in the following areas: store leadership, distribution center leadership, pharmacy, corporate undergraduate and corporate MBA opportunities

Tesla Motors Internship
Website:
https://www.tesla.com/careers/search/?query=internship&country=US

Requirements:

- Supply Chain-Logistics Internship is available to current undergraduate, graduate or MBA student
- Focus on supply chain management, business administration, engineering management, or UX/UI design
- Must have 3+ internship, project, or work experience related to this area of expertise, ability to effectively communicate verbally, and excellent time management skills.

TikTok Internship
Website: https://careers.tiktok.com/position/

Requirements:

- College student pursuing a degree in marketing/PR, communications, business, finance, design, etc.
- Understand digital media landscape

TransUnion LLC Internship
Website: https://www.transunion.com/about-us/careers

Requirements:

- College student with bachelor's degree in progress
- Excellent writing and communication skills
- Ability to organize and multi-task project requests, work well in a team environment as well as work independently

Travelers Insurance Pre-Finance Internship
Website:
https://careers.travelers.com/students-grads/internships/

Requirements:

- Undergraduate student who obtained or is pursuing a bachelor's or master's degree
- Sophomore (rising junior) majoring in finance and/or accounting
- Minimum 3.0 GPA

Walmart Merchandising Operations MBA Internship
Website: https://careers.walmart.com/students

Requirements:

- Option 1: Bachelor's degree in business, merchandising, or related field
- Option 2: Two years' experience in merchandising, buying, financial planning, operations, or related area

WarnerMedia Internship
Website:
https://careers.wbd.com/global/en/wbd-internships-early-careers

Requirements:

- Interested in the fields of technology, design, distribution, marketing, publicity, development, journalism, editorial, production, news, games, or animation
- Currently enrolled in a college degree program as an undergraduate, graduate, law school, or MBA student for the full duration of the internship

- Must be able to provide legal proof of eligibility to work in the U.S.
- Must be self-motivated, have the ability to work in a team environment and have a good attitude

Washington Performing Arts Internship
Website:
https://www.washingtonperformingarts.org/aboutus/internships/

Requirements:

- Highly motivated, creative, and hard-working individual with an interest in all aspects of arts management
- Preferred that applicants have previous office experience, strong organizational skills, effecting writing and communication skills, computer literary, and the ability to learn quickly

CHAPTER 12

DEVELOP YOUR POST-AWARD STRATEGY

Once your scholarship awards start rolling in, you may believe your work is done. However, there are still a variety of tasks that are required to complete the scholarship process.

First, you should promptly return or submit any forms that need to be completed and signed. Most scholarship awards have to be accepted in writing for the process to be finalized.

Second, be sure to formally thank the organization that awarded the scholarship. This should be done either with a formal letter through snail mail or a formal email. Informal communication for this purpose should be avoided, including text messages, phone calls, or impromptu email messages that are not professionally structured. You will want the sponsoring organization to have an official record of your statement of gratitude.

Some scholarship organizations may request that you submit thank you letters to their sponsors, or that you complete surveys about the scholarship experience or your educational achievements. Be sure to comply with all requests.

Third, maintain copies of all formal award documents in a file or computer folder, including the award letter and any supporting documentation. If you used a filing system while performing your scholarship research, you may include the information in the same file used to retain the application information. These items will likely be needed later to send to the educational institution's financial aid or admissions department. The arrival of funds often does not occur until after the next semester commences, or even later, and the documentation will serve as proof that arrival of the funds is imminent.

Fourth, keep track of each scholarship and the amount awarded in a spreadsheet program, like Excel. In my file, I used the headings Name of Scholarship, Amount, Deadline Date, Date of Submission, Date of Notification, Win/Lose. Tabulate the total amount received to ensure that your records correspond with those maintained by the college/university.

Fifth, add the scholarship(s) you received to the "Honors and Awards" section of your resume. Being a scholarship recipient offers a certain level of prestige, one that will be noticed by future employers and other key decision makers.

In fact, as your list of scholarship awards expands you will be afforded other promising career opportunities, such as internships and inclusion in leadership conferences. These opportunities will not only provide additional college funds but set you apart from other college graduates when you submit applications for professional career positions.

Next, review the information for all of the scholarships for which you submitted applications to determine which ones you can submit applications to for the following academic year. For those scholarships that sent you letters of regret, do not let the fact that you did not receive the scholarship the first time deter you from applying in the future. Often, the second time around will reap some rewards simply because you are already familiar with the process. A second application should be superior to the first, and you might receive a positive response the second time around.

In addition, some of the awards you receive may be renewable annually. Some may automatically renew if you meet certain criteria, such as a minimum grade point average and continued enrollment in a four-year institution. Maintaining the information about both types of scholarships separately will help you to keep track of re-submissions for the coming years.

Continue to research and pursue scholarship opportunities, even after you have reached your goal and received awards to cover your expenses. According to the College Board, the cost of college tuition is increasing annually at the rate of 3 percent.[22] It is a near certainty that your funding needs will increase from one year to the next, so it is best to be prepared for this likely occurrence.

Finally, share the information you have learned with others who desire to attend college debt-free. When students graduate with zero or minimal debt, the overall health of the American economy is strengthened. Those students will be able to purchase homes, automobiles, and other major items, and build savings accounts much sooner without the proverbial albatross of monthly student loan payments around their necks. They will not have the constant pressure of a seemingly never-ending balance due because most of their student loan payments go toward interest, not the principal. That is the ultimate purpose of this book: To help thousands of students across America and the world to obtain a debt-free college education.

ABOUT THE AUTHOR

Gwen Richardson has been a writer and entrepreneur for more than 30 years. She is the author of fifteen published books.

As her daughter's college years approached, she began researching scholarship opportunities and became passionate about the issue of college loan debt. As a result, her daughter attended all four years at an out-of-state university and graduated with zero college loan debt. Ms. Richardson's passion led to a desire to champion the cause of a debt-free college education for students across the United States, and she is a frequent speaker to youth groups and non-profit organizations on the subject of scholarships and college loans. *101 Scholarship Applications* was nominated for a 2015 NAACP Image Award. This book was originally published in 2014 and a revised edition is published in January of each year.

A long-time entrepreneur and a graduate of Georgetown University, Ms. Richardson currently resides in Houston, Texas, with her husband, Willie, and adult daughter, Sylvia. Communication via email is welcome, including speaking requests, at gwenrichardson123@gmail.com.

Visit the author's website: www.gwenrichardson.com

Alphabetical Index of Scholarships and Internships

OTHER BOOKS BY GWEN RICHARDSON

(Kindle version also available)

Kidz Biz is a children's book series that targets children ages 5 to 8. The three main characters in the series, Daisy, Robert, and Karim, are known as the Kidz Biz Squad. These three neighborhood kids develop witty business ideas to earn money for fun toys, trips, projects, and prizes. Each book in the series covers a different business concept or aspect of running a business. Children who read the books will learn the importance of finances, friendship, and fortitude. 40 pp. $12.00 for each installment.

Write It Right: The Guide to Self-Publishing Your Best Book provides both aspiring and seasoned authors with a road map to success. 142 pp. $12.00

You Are Wonderfully Made: 12 Life-Changing Principles for Teen Girls to Embrace empowers teen girls with the tools they need to successfully navigate their teen years and avoid the pitfalls that can derail their futures. They can be adopted by any teen girl, regardless of her family background, economic status, ethnicity, or educational achievement level. 94 pp. $10.00

The Genesis Files is the first book in a mystery/thriller series whose main character Lloyd Palmer. Palmer's job as a reporter for the Houston *Ledger* should have fulfilled his lifelong dream of being a journalist. But, along with being exhausted from the daily coverage of murders and mayhem in the nation's fourth largest city, he's hit a glass ceiling at work, and his editor, Ed Jackson, goes out of his way to make Lloyd's life miserable. While interviewing potential witnesses to a murder-suicide at a Houston high-rise, Lloyd meets a mysterious stranger who subsequently changes his life. But peril awaits as both he and his family barely escape a hired assassin. (Also read the book's sequel, *Exodus From Treachery*.) 300 pp. $15.00

Autographed copies of all titles by Gwen Richardson can be ordered via her web site: www.gwenrichardson.com

Copies can also be ordered by calling Cushcity Communications at its toll-free number: 1-800-340-5454

Other online source for purchase: www.amazon.com

END NOTES

[1] Information from Harvard Financial Aid Office on Harvard University website, www.college.harvard.edu., Accessed Nov. 28, 2022.
[2] Melanie Hanson, "Student Loan Debt Statistics," October 26, 2022, EducationData.org, Accessed Nov. 28, 2022.
[3] Ron Lieber and Tara Siegel Bernard, "For Millions Deep in Student Loan Debt, Bankruptcy Is No Easy Fix," Nov. 7, 2020, *The New York Times*, www.nytimes.com, Accessed Nov. 7, 2020.
[4] Delano R. Franklin and Samuel W. Zwickel, "Record-Low 4.59 Percent of Applicants Accepted to Harvard Class of 2022," *The Harvard Crimson*, www.thecrimson.com, Accessed Dec. 6, 2018.
[5] Coca-Cola Scholars Foundation, https://www.coca-colascholarsfoundation.org/blog/2020-semifinalists/, Accessed January 14, 2020.
[6] Lorena Roberts, "How to Pay Off Your Student Loans Faster," *College Campus Life News*, www.uloop.com, Accessed Jan. 4, 2018.
[7] Herrera, 2014.
[8] "The U.S. Department of Education offers low-interest loans to eligible students to help cover the cost of college or career school," www.studentaid.ed.gov, Accessed Nov. 14, 2019.
[9] Robert Farrington, "As Graduate School Student Loan Debt Balloons, It's Time to Implement Borrowing Caps," Nov. 25, 2022, *Forbes*, www.forbes.com, Accessed Nov. 29, 2022.
[10] Dell Scholars Program, http://www.dellscholarsprogram.org/scholarship/overview, Accessed Aug. 23, 2014
[11] Lynnette Khalfani Cox, "5 College Scholarship Scams to Avoid," July 21, 2014, *Ebony*, www.ebony.com, Accessed Sept. 9, 2014
[12] Internal Revenue Service, Publication 970, Tax Benefits for Education, www.irs.gov
[13] U.S. Department of Education website, https://studentaid.ed.gov/fafsa, Accessed Sept. 6, 2014
[14] Elizabeth Hoyt, "President Obama Announces Changes to 2017-2018 FAFSA," Sept. 17, 2015, Fastweb.com, http://www.fastweb.com/financial-aid/articles/President-Obama-Announces-Changes-to-2017-18-FAFSA, Accessed Sept. 23, 2015
[15] Herrera, 2014.
[16] Herrera, 2014.
[17] Elizabeth Hoyt, "Crowdfunding for college," Sept. 11, 2013,

---

Fastweb.com, http://www.fastweb.com/financial-aid/articles/4035-crowdfunding-for-college, Accessed Sept. 5, 2014

[18] Andrew Josuweit, "5 Crowdfunding Sites That Will Destroy Your Student Loan Debt," *Forbes*, May 2, 2018, www.forbes.com, Accessed May 2, 2018.

[19] Andrew Josuweit, 2018.

[20] Andrew Josuweit, 2018.

[21] Hoyt, 2013

[22] "Trends in Higher Education: Average Rates of Growth of Published Charges by Decade," College Board, https://trends.collegeboard.org/college-pricing/figures-tables/average-rates-growth-tuition-and-fees-over-time, Accessed Sept. 2, 2014

Made in the USA
Monee, IL
04 November 2026

67378950R00144